Autonomous Vehicles
The Road to Economic Growth?

Autonomous Vehicles

The Road to Economic Growth?

CLIFFORD WINSTON

QUENTIN KARPILOW

Brookings Institution Press

Washington, D.C.

Library of Congress Control Number: 2020936118
ISBN 9780815738572 (pbk : alk. paper)
ISBN 9780815738589 (ebook)

9 8 7 6 5 4 3 2 1

Typeset in Maiola

Composition by Elliott Beard

Contents

Part 3
Constraints on the Success of Autonomous Vehicles

Acknowledgments

We are grateful to Edward Glaeser and José A. Gómez-Ibáñez for initial collaboration on a submission to the Wolfson Economics Prize, which included some of the material in this book. We also received useful comments and suggestions from Stephanie Aaronson, Martin Adler, Alan Blinder, Marlon Boarnet, Robert Crandall, Matthew Kahn, Ashley Langer, Paul Lewis, Shanjun Li, Robin Lindsey, Vikram Maheshri, Fred Mannering, Ashley Nunes, James Sallee, Marc Scribner, Chad Shirley, Kenneth Small, Mike Smart, and Jia Yan.

Katherine Kimball carefully edited the manuscript, Cecilia González managed the editorial production process, and Enid Zafran created the index.

Part 1

Introduction and Background

1

Introduction

Transportation innovations and investments have contributed significantly to U.S. economic growth. They have enabled households to optimize their residential and workplace locations and their choice of employers; encouraged firms to increase the size and scope of their markets, reduce their inventories, and expand their choice of workers; and allowed consumers to benefit from greater competition among domestic and international firms and from more product variety. The motor vehicle, which has contributed greatly to those socially desirable activities, has been listed among the greatest human inventions of all time (Bowler 2017; Winston 2010).

The increasing dominance of cars and trucks for transporting passengers and freight has evolved with the development of the U.S. public road system, which represents the nation's largest civilian public investment and has become the arterial network of the U.S. economy. Today, some 90 percent of commuters use cars to get to work, 70 percent of travelers use cars for intercity trips, and 30 percent of shippers of intercity freight (measured in ton-miles) and nearly all of their urban freight is shipped by truck—all of those movements rely on a federal-highway capital stock that is valued at roughly $3 trillion (Winston 2013).[1]

Given the importance for the U.S. economy of motor-vehicle transportation and the infrastructure that it uses, significant changes in the performance of either could have a large effect on economic growth. To date, however, the road network has been characterized by growing traffic congestion, deteriorating pavement, crumbling bridges, and a staggering number of crashes. The annual cost of congestion, vehicle damage, and injuries and fatalities runs in the trillions of dollars.

Some economists have argued that the decades-long underfunding of highway infrastructure is the cause of those problems. They have called for policymakers to increase expenditures to repair pavement, renovate bridges, build new roads, and modernize signaling.[2] Other economists have highlighted the inefficiencies in government highway pricing and investment policy, arguing that the public sector has wasted hundreds of billions of dollars by failing to charge road users for their contribution to congestion and their damage to pavement and bridges and by neglecting to make investments that maximize social benefits.[3]

Those calls for reform have largely gone unanswered. Federal efforts to improve our nation's highway system have stalled for decades. Although nineteen states have raised their gasoline taxes since 2015, they have done so only because improvements in the fuel economy of the nation's automobile fleet—together with a federal gasoline tax that has been fixed at its 1993 level of 18.4 cents per gallon—have led to shortfalls in federal money available from the federal Highway Trust Fund (Langer, Maheshri, and Winston 2017).[4] Both major political parties agree that the United States has been experiencing an infrastructure crisis for years. However, they have yet to take any major steps to address it.

The Emergence and Potential of Autonomous Vehicles

Notwithstanding those bleak conditions, there is still hope for the highway transportation system. Self-driving or autonomous vehicles, a long-awaited catalyst for change, are quickly emerging from the private sector. As this book argues, autonomous vehicles represent a watershed moment in the development of transportation. If properly encouraged, this innovation promises not only to vastly improve road travel and generate huge benefits to travelers, shippers, and delivery companies but also to benefit the entire economy by reducing congestion and virtually eliminating vehicle accidents. In addition, although autonomous vehicles' effects on land use, employment, other modes of travel, and public finance are likely to be mixed, the negative effects are generally overstated, because they ignore plausible adjustments by the public and policymakers that could ameliorate them.

As Bowler (2017) notes in the case of air transportation, as late as the 1920s skeptics still scoffed at the whole idea of a commercially viable aviation industry. Rapid technical developments soon allowed their arguments to be discounted. Still, as late as 1937, Sir Harold Harley told a BBC audience that no major innovations could be foreseen in aviation technology (Bowler 2017).

Similarly, autonomous vehicles have attracted vocal naysayers, who assert that the technology may never work effectively enough to improve highway transportation significantly or that it will take a long time before those vehicles are in regular use and that even then, they are likely to increase road travel and to worsen congestion. Litman (2019) summarizes various doubts about autonomous vehicles. The popular press also feeds negative views with pieces titled "Cars Are Death Machines. Self-Driving Tech Won't Change That" (Arieff 2019) and "Silicon Valley Pioneered Self-Driving Cars. But Some of Its Tech Savvy Residents Don't Want Them Tested in Their Neighborhoods" (Siddiqui 2019).

We and others are optimistic about the likely success of autonomous vehicles in the long run for a number of reasons. The competition and cooperation that is evolving in the autonomous-vehicle industry is unprecedented in its global scope. The technology has greatly progressed and continues to advance at a rapid rate. The incentives for industry participants to succeed and the cost of failure are enormous. And it is plausible that competition among cities, states, and even countries will develop and provide incentives for policymakers to enact policies that expedite the adoption and efficient operations of autonomous vehicles.

Nonetheless, doubters are likely to modify their views only if and when autonomous vehicles are widely adopted and are operating safely and efficiently. In the meantime, policy analysts can play an important and constructive role by identifying and analyzing some important policy issues that must be addressed effectively to ensure that autonomous vehicles will be safe and efficient when the public begins to adopt them to replace nonautonomous vehicles.

A Global Effort

In 2011 two top engineers for Google traveled to Detroit in the hope of working with a car company to build and sell a fleet of self-driving cars (Burns and Shulgan 2018). But when no one in Detroit was interested, Google (and subsequently Waymo, its self-driving car project) took the lead in introducing autonomous vehicles to the world. A few years later, U.S. and foreign automakers, other technology firms, and various start-up ventures were in hot pursuit, either by themselves or in a partnership.[5] Now, nearly all major car companies in the world, as well as technology, cargo, and startup companies, are engaged in developing autonomous vehicles.[6] Hundreds more companies have emerged to develop various components of the technology.

Various partnerships between foreign firms, governments and firms, and universities and firms abound. Waymo has struck a deal with Renault-Nissan to bring driverless cars to Japan and France; Ford and Argo.ai are in talks with Volkswagen about building self-driving car fleets; GM Cruise is partnering with Honda; Uber is growing closer with Toyota; and Fiat-Chrysler and Amazon are partnering with Aurora. China and South Korea have indicated their intention to support the efforts of their companies to become world leaders in autonomous-vehicle technology and adoption. Other countries are likely to follow suit. And America's leading technology universities, including but not limited to MIT and Carnegie Mellon, are aiding the autonomous-vehicle industry by researching ways to improve the vehicles' performance in complex driving environments and by training the computer-science talent that the industry is employing.[7]

Today, total global investment in autonomous-vehicle technology exceeds $100 billion, and that figure is increasing rapidly as competition intensifies (Kerry and Karsten 2017). For example, Hyundai announced that it is planning to invest some $35 billion in autonomous-vehicle technology by 2025.[8] Atkinson and Foote (2018) notes that global growth in autonomous vehicles is expected to be fastest in North America. Foreign automakers and technology companies have been investing in U.S.-based R&D and are locating in the United States, underscoring U.S. leadership in this emerging field.

At the same time, countries throughout the world are investing in infrastructure to facilitate autonomous vehicles production and adoption. China is building a new highway with dedicated lanes for autonomous vehicles that will be used by their leading autonomous-vehicle companies, Baidu, Pony.ai, and WeRide. The highway connects Beijing and the Xiong'an New Area in Hebei Province, some sixty miles away. In addition, China's leading telecommunications equipment manufacturer, Huawei, is building technology that could take on a large part of the processing required to run an autonomous vehicle.

Although firms are partnering with one another, they are also competing intensely to offer a reliable autonomous vehicle to the public because their very existence is at stake. In the United States, General Motors survived even though the Chevrolet Bolt was not the successful electric vehicle it had hoped for, while Tesla developed an electric vehicle that is selling nearly 200,000 units annually. However, General Motors and Ford will face much more competition in the market for autonomous vehicles, with far greater implications for their market shares. These companies are transforming themselves by closing plants that produce passenger cars, slashing their workforce to save billions of dollars annually, and using these savings to invest in new technologies that they hope will propel them to the forefront of the autonomous-vehicle industry of the future.[9] Although the U.S. government has helped domestic automakers in the past by providing them with bailouts and protection from foreign competition, financial assistance will not transform a U.S. firm that falls behind in the highly competitive global autonomous-vehicle industry into an industry leader, and it is therefore unlikely to be provided by the government.[10]

As a result of industry competition and cooperation, vehicle technology is progressing at such a rapid rate that the relevant question in America is no longer whether its surface-transportation system will be made up entirely of autonomous vehicles in the foreseeable future. The question is when will the transformation occur. And that question cannot be addressed without understanding the pervasive role of government in the adoption process.

In any case, recent testing has moved beyond operating the vehicle in good weather and in a low-risk environment to identifying and overcoming atypical but challenging conditions that could arise in practice, such as driving in blinding snow and combating terrorists' efforts to cause a vehicle to crash into other vehicles or to run over pedestrians. In addition, automobile and technology companies are developing the capacity to promptly fix any technical problems in their autonomous-vehicle fleets, and they are increasingly aware of the liability issues that surround autonomous vehicles.

The Role of Government

Government policymakers do not simply need to stay out of the way to facilitate autonomous vehicle transportation. They must take a number of important steps, which include establishing a framework for vehicle testing and conditions for adoption, making appropriate investments in highway-network technology to facilitate communication between autonomous vehicles and between such vehicles and highway infrastructure and operators, and reforming pricing and investment policies to enable the safe and efficient operation of autonomous vehicles.

Accordingly, policymakers pose a greater risk than industry participants regarding when, if ever, U.S. society realizes the huge potential benefits of autonomous vehicles. They could delay implementing guidelines for testing of autonomous vehicles and ensuring their timely adoption. They could put off the costly investments in technology that facilitate communications between vehicles and from vehicle to infrastructure and network, some of which public authorities will have to install and manage effectively to facilitate mass use of autonomous vehicles on the U.S. road system. And they could fail to remedy inefficiencies in highway-infrastructure pricing, investment, and production policy, which have compromised nonautonomous-vehicle travel for decades and must be reformed to enable autonomous vehicles to operate efficiently and to raise revenue from highway users to help finance the investments in new infrastructure technology.[11]

A Brief Roadmap

The main purpose of this book is to present an overview of the potential benefits of autonomous vehicles, providing empirical estimates wherever possible, and to assess the current technological challenges and public-policy concerns. Its goal is to encourage industry participants and policymakers to make constructive use of the time between the current period, when autonomous vehicles are being tested in selected locales, and the transition period, when the public starts to adopt autonomous vehicles for their actual travel, to significantly address the potential problems. Although the book focuses primarily on the United States, the substantive and policy issues raised here are relevant for all countries that seek to adopt autonomous vehicles expeditiously and successfully.

This book draws three primary conclusions.

The potential benefits from autonomous vehicles are extensive and enormous. In particular, the benefits to the economy from reducing congestion could raise annual economic growth by at least 1 percentage point. In addition, the gains from virtually eliminating fatalities, injuries, and collision damage would be very large. Finally, the alleged costs of autonomous vehicles in terms of land use, employment, other modes of transportation, and public finance are likely to be overstated. In fact, they could be turned into positive effects through plausible adjustments by the public (for example, in housing and labor markets) and through the implementation of efficient public policies by transportation officials.

The major obstacles to realizing most of the potential benefits are primarily policy related, rather than technological. The federal government has already delayed vehicle testing and adoption, and it seems unable to understand that current inefficiencies in highway policy pose a serious threat to the success of autonomous vehicles. Some local and state governments have shown an interest in upgrading their infrastructure technology so that their roads could be used efficiently by autonomous vehicles, but they have not turned their attention to reforming inefficient highway policies.

In the long run, despite the failure of policymakers to implement efficient highway infrastructure policies in the past, competitive forces at the city, state, and even country level may spur policymakers to reform their highway policies to enhance autonomous vehicle operations. Given that policymakers have time to adjust their policies, cautious optimism that trillion-dollar bills will not be left on the sidewalk in the coming decades is warranted.

As this book went to press, a global pandemic had broken out, caused by a coronavirus (COVID-19) that was first detected in Wuhan, China. The outbreak quickly manifested an unforeseen benefit of autonomous vehicles by spurring China to expedite production and adoption of autonomous delivery services provided by small vans. Autonomous delivery services enabled medical providers and consumers to reduce their human exposure and address labor shortages caused by quarantines. As the coronavirus spread to the United States and other countries, public health professionals stressed the importance of "social distancing"—maintaining physical distance from others—to curb the virus's spread and to "flatten the curve," meaning that people would become infected more gradually, thus preventing surges in the need for medical services that would overwhelm hospitals. In the short run, autonomous vehicle companies are likely to focus more of their efforts on autonomous deliveries. In a post-coronavirus world, autonomous vehicles carrying passengers and cargo will gain significant attention as a vital way to flatten the curve associated with future viruses and to reduce the disruption of economic and other activities. Accordingly, the book's focus on governments taking actions to expedite the adoption and efficient use of autonomous vehicles has even greater urgency and importance.

Part 1 of this book discusses autonomous vehicle operations and the process of vehicle adoption. The various potential effects of autonomous vehicles on travel conditions and the economic environment are addressed in part 2. Given autonomous vehicles' potential to reduce congestion, and the difficulty of establishing a causal relationship between congestion and various economic performance measures, we devote considerable attention to developing and executing an approach to provide a rough estimate of the effect that autonomous vehicles could have on economic growth by reducing congestion. Congestion is an important example of a negative effect of traditional or nonautonomous vehicles that autonomous vehicles could reduce. We also discuss the other negative effects of automobiles that autonomous vehicles could reduce, including threats to travelers' health and safety, and examine how autonomous vehicles could affect accessibility, land use, the overall U.S. transportation system, employment, and public finance. Finally, in part 3 we assess the technological and public-policy issues that could impede the success of autonomous vehicles and draw preliminary conclusions about whether competition among cities, states, and countries to enable consumers to realize the benefits of autonomous vehicles could influence policymakers to address those issues adequately.

2

Autonomous-Vehicle Operations and the Process of Adoption

The Society of Automotive Engineers has created a widely accepted scale of vehicle autonomy, which ranges from level 0 (no autonomy) to level 5 (cars that do not need a steering wheel or pedals because they can perform the entire trip without human input). Motorists have already grown accustomed to some level of independence from their cars. Many vehicles, for instance, have collision-avoidance systems or self-parking features that place them at a level 1 on the scale.

To take just one example, the 2018 Mercedes-Benz S-Class advertises its vehicles as having a suite of safety and driver-assistive technologies, including a detection system that autonomously brakes if a pedestrian or bicyclist gets in front of the car; a lane-monitoring system that steers the vehicle between the lines on the road; a lane-changing function that is activated on command; and automatic speed control that reads current road conditions and adjusts to the conditions ahead. Finally, the vehicle is equipped with a car-to-car communication feature that enables similarly equipped Mercedes vehicles to send one another warning messages about road conditions, such as icy patches to avoid, the location of a tree blocking the road, or an accident delaying traffic.

This is not to suggest that all the engineering challenges to achieving level-5 operations have been solved—or are even close to being solved. Nor does it imply that the benefits from autonomous vehicles discussed in this book could be achieved only with level-5 autonomous vehicles. Level-4 autonomous vehicles (which are self-driving but operate only under well-specified conditions, such as certain road types or geographic areas) could also provide significant benefits. However, because we take a long-run view of autonomous-vehicle development, testing, and adoption, our main focus here is on level-5 vehicles.

In theory, a vehicle operating at level 5 is likely to draw on a combination of technologies to drive itself, as illustrated in figure 2-1. Sensors on board the vehicle use radio waves (radar), light waves (light detection and ranging, or LIDAR), and photography to measure the distance of the car from various objects, such as pedestrians, bicyclists, and other cars. An onboard computer processes this and other information noted below in real time and executes plans to proceed safely toward the vehicle's destination. Figure 2-2 illustrates what the car sees so it can operate in traffic. The global positioning system (GPS), supplemented with highly detailed digital maps, locates the vehicle that has the right-of-way. Communications between vehicles (V2V) and between vehicles and roadway infrastructure (V2I) help inform cars of the location and intentions of other vehicles as well as the condition of the roadway and the status of traffic signals.

Improving the Technology and Overcoming Challenges

Automakers, technology companies, and research universities are continuing to explore ways that autonomous vehicles could be improved to operate safely in all driving conditions and in response to all behaviors they are likely to encounter, including individuals driving nonautonomous vehicles, pedestrians, and bicyclists. According to the Department of Transportation secretary Elaine Chao, more than 1,400 self-driving cars, trucks, and other vehicles are currently

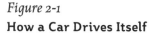

Figure 2-1

How a Car Drives Itself

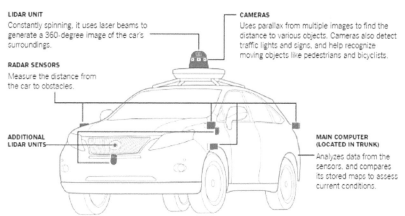

LIDAR UNIT
Constantly spinning, it uses laser beams to generate a 360-degree image of the car's surroundings.

RADAR SENSORS
Measure the distance from the car to obstacles.

CAMERAS
Uses parallax from multiple images to find the distance to various objects. Cameras also detect traffic lights and signs, and help recognize moving objects like pedestrians and bicyclists.

ADDITIONAL LIDAR UNITS

MAIN COMPUTER (LOCATED IN TRUNK)
Analyzes data from the sensors, and compares its stored maps to assess current conditions.

Note: Car is a Lexus model modified by Google. SOURCE: GOOGLE, GUILBERT GATES/THE NEW YORK TIMES

in testing by more than eighty companies across thirty-six states and the District of Columbia.[1] Generally, the industry has evolved to combine a simulation approach and a vehicle-miles-driven approach to testing and improving vehicles, which allows for more testing in a wider variety of driving environments.

For example, Waymo, Alphabet's self-driving-car unit, is using simulation to teach its autonomous vehicles how to respond to a situation that they have not encountered before. Once a car actually drives and redrives that specific situation and its many variations, the skill is added to its knowledge base and shared with Waymo's network of self-driving cars. Researchers are also teaching self-driving cars to recognize and predict pedestrian movements with great precision by creating a "biomechanically inspired recurrent neural network" that catalogs human movements.[2] With this capability, the cars can predict poses and future locations for one or several pedestrians up to fifty yards from the vehicle.

Some companies, such as Aeva, are developing next-generation

Figure 2-2
What the Car Sees

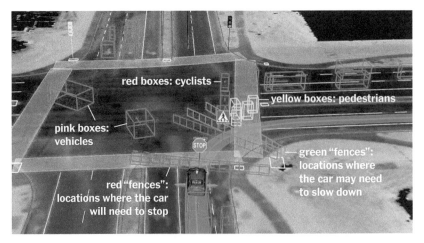

red boxes: cyclists

yellow boxes: pedestrians

pink boxes: vehicles

green "fences": locations where the car may need to slow down

red "fences": locations where the car will need to stop

Note: The car sensors gather data on nearby objects, such as their size and rate of speed, if any. The sensors categorize the objects—as cyclists, pedestrians, or other cars and objects—based on how they behave and transmit signals as to how to respond. SOURCE: GOOGLE, GUILBERT GATES/THE NEW YORK TIMES

LIDAR, which can more accurately measure a car's distance from surrounding objects (pedestrians, cyclists, and other vehicles) and the velocity of those objects and predict the future motion of those objects with less prediction error. Luminar is developing a LIDAR technology that can detect whether a pedestrian, for example, is on his or her phone and not paying attention to roadway conditions; this facility provides an additional visual cue that an autonomous vehicle could use to make decisions, such as whether to slow down. New artificial-intelligence cameras enable autonomous vehicles to recognize images much faster and to make quicker decisions, and the next generation of LIDAR sensors is being collapsed to a single chip, which will greatly reduce its cost by facilitating mass production and by reducing moving parts that may break. Finally, Nvidia Corporation has built a powerful new computer, code-named Pegasus, capable of quickly processing information on a nonautonomous vehicle's surrounding environment, enabling the vehicle to operate safely as a fully autonomous vehicle.

Certain industry participants are taking steps to address LIDAR's shortcomings in specific environments and situations. For example, LIDAR does not detect black cars as well as it sees vehicles of other colors. PPG Industries has therefore developed a paint that allows the near-infrared light emitted by lasers to pass through a dark car's exterior and to rebound off a reflective undercoat, making it visible to sensors. The company is also developing other coatings to improve sensors' abilities when their performance is reduced by dirt and ice. In addition, LIDAR has difficulties measuring distances between objects in whiteout conditions. An autonomous car developed in Finland, Martti, is using a newly developed radar system to enable it to drive safely on snow-covered roads, and WaveSense, a Boston-area start-up, has developed a ground-penetrating radar system to keep autonomous vehicles on the road regardless of the weather. Finally, the MIT Media Lab is developing a new imaging system that can gauge the distance of objects obscured by thick fog.

Autonomous vehicles currently rely on either highly detailed 3D maps that tell the system what to expect or well-marked lanes that they can navigate in an urban or highway environment. But many roads are not paved with lane markings or have not been 3D-mapped in detail. Mack (2018) reports that MIT has begun to address this limitation by developing MapLite, which combines GPS, using only the most basic topographical maps from OpenStreetMap, with LIDAR and IMU (inertial measurement unit) sensors that monitor road conditions. In addition, Mississippi State University's Center for Advanced Vehicular Systems has developed a simulator to collect data to help autonomous vehicles recognize realistic off-road landscapes; it is also developing a test track for off-road vehicle testing.[3]

Keeping abreast of the latest driving challenges that industry participants have identified and their latest technological approaches for overcoming them can be a challenge. Although the industry has certainly not resolved all of the problems facing autonomous vehicles, neither has it exhausted all technological solutions; in fact, it continues to explore new ones, as the following examples illustrate. Until now, four kinds of sensors—video cameras, radar, ultrasonic sensors, and LIDAR—have been used to enable autonomous vehicles to perceive the objects around them so that they are sufficiently safe. But deficiencies still exist in the sensor suite, such as distance limitations and reduced perception in heavy rain (Quain 2019). LIDAR companies are working on higher-wavelength models that could provide longer-range, highway-speed systems that see through rain and snow. Radar companies are also working on improvements, such as 4D imaging radar that can create detailed images at distances of more than 900 feet. A possible solution that goes beyond those improvements may be far-infrared cameras (thermal cameras), which detect wavelengths below the visible spectrum that indicate heat. Companies have been developing infrared cameras for various military applications and rescue operations, and some have recently put infrared sensors on autonomous vehicles to explore and demonstrate their capabilities.

Generally, industry participants have been proactive in establishing safety principles and guidelines, which should become part of a framework that is eventually instituted by government regulators to set national safety standards for autonomous vehicles. In April 2016, Ford, Lyft, Uber, Volvo, and Waymo initiated the Self-Driving Coalition for Safer Streets. Recently, eleven companies proposed guiding principles for self-driving vehicles for the development, testing, and validation of safe autonomous vehicles.[4] Those initiatives indicate that industry and academic researchers worldwide are committed to improving the safety of autonomous vehicles collaboratively and strongly suggest that their efforts will eventually coalesce to perfect those vehicles for safe use by the traveling public.

Potential Travel Improvements

Autonomous-vehicle technology has the potential to significantly improve the safety, speed, reliability, and cost of road travel in four ways. It can prevent collisions—94 percent of which, according to the National Highway Traffic Safety Administration, are caused by human error[5]—and thereby greatly reduce highway fatalities, serious injuries, vehicle damage, and costly insurance by gathering and reacting immediately to real-time information and by eliminating concerns about risky human behavior, such as distracted and impaired driving. It can significantly reduce both recurrent and incident delays and improve travel time reliability by reducing accidents and, when necessary, by rerouting drivers who have programmed their destinations.[6] It can allow vehicles to travel closer together and at higher speeds more safely by creating a smoother traffic flow, thereby effectively increasing highway capacity without the public having to incur the enormous cost of building and maintaining additional lanes and new freeways. And it can reduce the cost of chauffeured passenger, for-hire trucking, and postal services by eliminating the need for a driver.[7]

Finally, by smoothing traffic flow and reducing stop-and-go driving, autonomous vehicles will achieve improved fuel economy and, in combination with the development of electric vehicles (EVs), could significantly reduce pollution and improve the environment. Companies' development and commercialization of EVs is currently proceeding independently of the development and commercialization of AVs; it is expected that EVs and AVs will be combined eventually and that the resulting autonomous electric vehicles (AEVs) will eliminate the social costs of tailpipe emissions, which are expected to exceed the social cost of generating electricity for EVs, by replacing gasoline-powered nonautonomous vehicles.

Connectedness

The ability to drive itself, or automation, is clearly a critical feature of an autonomous vehicle. But the other critical feature is its connectedness to other vehicles and their surroundings, including pedestrians, infrastructure, and the network, which allows for the optimization of the vehicular system as a whole. Connectedness is achieved by various communication models, summarized by Mutschler (2018) as follows:

- vehicle to infrastructure (V2I), which includes communications to traffic-signal timing, speeds limits, prioritization, and traffic signs (for example, changing traffic signal lights)

- vehicle to vehicle (V2V), which enables collision avoidance (for example, ambulance approaching)

- vehicle to pedestrian (V2P), which can transmit safety alerts to pedestrians and cyclists (for example, vehicle approaching, pedestrian crossing street ahead)

- vehicle to network (V2N), which enables communication about real time traffic, work zones, routing, and cloud services (for example, traffic congestion two miles ahead)

Policymakers must engage with the autonomous-vehicle industry to determine the appropriate investments that could enable autonomous vehicles to operate safely and efficiently in their states and cities with the essential communication capabilities.

Incentives for Automakers and Technology Companies

Chris Urmson, the former director of self-driving cars at Google, argues that the private sector has a financial incentive to expedite deployment of autonomous vehicles because it can earn revenues on a per mile rather than a per unit basis. He refers to the following equation to approximate the size of the industry based on revenue:

$$\text{3 trillion VMT} \times \$0.10 \text{ per mile} = \$300 \text{ billion per year,}$$

where VMT refers to annual vehicle miles traveled in the United States and travelers are charged $0.10 a mile to cover costs.

Bosch and others (2018) finds a somewhat higher cost figure, based on a review of academic empirical estimates of the cost per mile of autonomous vehicles that puts the cost in the range of $0.15–$0.20 per mile. In any case, Urmson offers a plausible hypothesis that travelers could reduce the capital costs of vehicle ownership, including insurance, by apportioning them over the number of miles driven by acquiring or sharing a vehicle through a "transportation subscription service."[8]

Automakers could then improve their earnings by selling the use of autonomous vehicles that consumers share through rentals or subscriptions instead of by selling a given volume of units. Individuals and households would operate autonomous vehicles as transportation as a service (TaaS).[9] For example, assuming, on average, that auto companies currently turn a profit of roughly $1,500 per car and that a car lasts 150,000 miles, then their profit is a penny per mile traveled, which is likely to be less than the profit per mile traveled that they could earn by charging consumers a per mile fee for a shared autonomous vehicle.[10] Of course, the extensive collaboration in the autonomous-vehicle industry, the reinvention that autonomous-vehicle providers will have to make in the way they market and differentiate services, and firms' extensive investments in R&D and their huge fixed costs suggest a high degree of uncertainty about the level and distribution of future profits.

Travelers' Incentives for Adoption

Adopting autonomous vehicles would also greatly benefit travelers. Small and Verhoef (2007) reports that the average cost of highway travel time and unreliability amounts to $0.40 per mile and that the average cost of accidents is $0.14 per mile. If travelers pay $0.10 per mile, or even somewhat more, for their autonomous-vehicle transportation, those costs are likely to be strongly offset by the benefits from reduced travel times and greater reliability and from the virtual elimination of accident costs.

The large benefits from this back-of-the-envelope calculation are consistent with Fagnant and Kockelman (2015), which accounts for the benefits from the reduction in vehicle accidents and travel delays under the assumption that autonomous vehicles would reduce freeway delays from 35 to 60 percent, depending on the extent of autonomous vehicle (AV) market penetration and accounting for the additional travel that the vehicles may induce that would increase congestion.[11]

Technologically, the large benefits accrued from reducing congestion derive from the basic relation, traffic flow = travel speed × traffic density. Consider the case of a traffic accident that creates significant congestion, as people rubber neck to view the incident, causing traffic to slow to a crawl. Autonomous vehicles could significantly increase travel flows in such situations because they could smooth traffic flow and travel closer together without jeopardizing safety and could maintain a more consistent speed by not slowing down to view the aftermath. As noted, incident delays account for roughly one-third of all delays, so even modest improvements in traffic flows from reducing those delays could amount to significant savings in time and reliability that could yield large social benefits. Of course, autonomous vehicles could also improve traffic flows by the same type of mechanism to reduce other types of delays.

Wu and others (2017) presents simulations to examine the impact that autonomous vehicles could have on improving traffic flows even in traffic that includes nonautonomous vehicles. Small experiments involving a few dozen cars on a closed circuit show that a single autonomous vehicle could reduce traffic congestion by subtly moderating the speed of every other car on the road. In larger simulations, once autonomous vehicles reach a level of 5 to 10 percent of all cars on the road, they can manage localized traffic in complex environments—such as when eight lanes of traffic merge into two or at an extremely busy intersection. An autonomous vehicle carefully increases the space between itself and the car ahead, anticipating that it will abruptly slow down at some point down the road. However, because the self-driving vehicle has created a buffer, it can keep driving at the same pace—avoiding the cascade effect that its own braking would have on the cars behind it. In time, a new equilibrium is reached where all the cars are moving at a steady pace.

Daziano, Sarrias, and Leard (2017) takes a different perspective on travelers' benefits from autonomous vehicles and finds that the average household's willingness to pay for those vehicles greatly exceeds the additional cost of the technology. To be sure, our rough calculation and the preceding studies should be qualified because the actual benefits of autonomous vehicles will depend on whether the government reforms policies that would enhance their driving environment and performance. They will also be affected by the extent to which travelers reduce the capital costs of vehicle ownership by sharing vehicles through transportation subscription services.

The Role of the Government

Applying autonomous-vehicle prototypes to multiple geographies is difficult because cities have different road infrastructures—from signs to road paint—and different norms that drivers follow. In addition, no public benchmarks exist for how autonomous vehicles should perform in a given scenario to meet a standard of safety. Accordingly, all levels of government have a critical role to play in the public's adoption of autonomous vehicles because the public highway infrastructure is provided by local, state, and federal governments and because the federal government is generally responsible for regulating motor-vehicle safety.

Other major innovations have also relied on infrastructure provided by the government. For example, cell phones and eventually smartphones relied on the government-provided electromagnetic spectrum to enable communication through cellular technology.

Similarly, autonomous vehicles must depend on the public road system to transport passengers and freight by vehicles that drive themselves. Because inefficient infrastructure policies have contributed to the large social costs of nonautonomous vehicle travel, it is important for policymakers to reform highway-infrastructure pricing, investment, and production policies to reduce those costs for autonomous-vehicle travel. In addition, local and state governments will need to make investments to upgrade the physical characteristics and communication capabilities of their infrastructure to facilitate autonomous-vehicle travel.

In 2018 Congress drafted but failed to pass important autonomous-vehicle legislation that would have clarified and expedited vehicle testing and possibly vehicle adoption. The House passed self-driving legislation, called the Self-Drive Act, but the Senate failed to pass its version, the AV Start Act. Five Democratic senators blocked floor consideration and a final vote on the bill, and Senate Majority Leader Mitch McConnell chose not to use up limited floor time by bringing a cloture motion to defeat the holds. As this book goes to press, Congress is considering but has failed to pass a revision of its autonomous vehicle legislation.

The National Highway Traffic Safety Administration (NHTSA) could have initiated motor-vehicle-safety rulemakings without additional federal legislation. The only step forward that NHTSA has taken was to approve in February 2020 its first exemption from safety standards for a self-driving car. The exemption is limited to Nuro's R2, which is not designed to carry people but instead to deliver groceries or pizza and to have a top speed of 25 miles per hour.

The purpose of the congressional acts was to mandate a conflicts audit and recommendations for future rulemaking amendments and additions and to greatly expand exempted annual vehicle volumes while future amendments and additions are being developed over the next decade. Given that NHTSA has not made any major rulemakings, it is important for Congress to pass autonomous-vehicle legislation to ensure that the agency takes appropriate actions in a timely fashion, to expedite regulatory development pertaining to vehicle design and performance, and to provide regulatory relief where appropriate. Specifically, the legislation would allow the secretary of transportation to provide regulatory exemptions for a maximum number of vehicles per automaker per year, thereby enabling automakers to test their vehicles without any delay in advance of NHTSA's setting the final standards through the Federal Motor Vehicle Safety Standards at some future date.[12]

Finally, new legislation would affirm federal responsibility for the safety of autonomous vehicles and would prevent states from instituting their own vehicle regulations beyond their normal responsibilities of licensing and registration. Thus automakers and technology companies would not have to navigate through a patchwork of different regulations to test their vehicles and could work with regulators both to determine the safety goals that their vehicles would be expected to achieve and to identify how those goals would be met.[13]

As is the case with nonautonomous vehicles, individual automakers would be required to ensure their compliance with the safety standards by self-certification. After NHTSA sets the final standards, makers of autonomous vehicles would be free to sell their vehicles to the public, and consumers would begin their transition from driving nonautonomous vehicles to traveling in autonomous vehicles. The public's adoption of autonomous vehicles would therefore occur after NHTSA had set its final design and performance standards, which could take several years, during which time agency officials observed automakers' testing of autonomous vehicles and improvements in the technology. Widespread adoption would only occur once the majority of travelers had purchased or arranged to share AVs and no longer use nonautonomous vehicles, which could take several more years. In sum, it could be at least fifteen to twenty years before the public's adoption of autonomous vehicles exceeds 50 percent, and it could be another ten years before autonomous vehicles are completely adopted and used throughout the country.[14] Of course, positive or negative government policy or nonpolicy shocks to the adoption process could alter that timetable.

In the absence of federal legislation that has affirmed the federal government's role in the testing and adoption process, some cities and states have started to pass their own regulations to allow testing of autonomous vehicles within their borders. The number of cities conducting or planning to conduct a test is steadily growing.[15] However, federal legislation must be passed to allow the formal adoption process to begin.[16]

Notwithstanding the delays in instituting federal regulations, autonomous-vehicle providers are already competing intensely in technology so that they can deploy their vehicles as soon as the federal legislation is passed, increasing the likelihood that they will survive the anticipated shakeout when final regulations are in place and consumers start to adopt autonomous vehicles. None of the autonomous-vehicle companies want to suffer the fate of Nokia and Blackberry, driven out of the market by a superior technology, Apple's iPhone, which was promptly introduced when the infrastructure, telecommunications bandwidth, could accommodate it and when new entry and intense competition ensued.

Certain countries, such as China, may be able to expedite public adoption of autonomous vehicles because its citizens are seemingly more trusting of the technology than are those of other countries and because the government can more easily overcome political obstacles when it wants to initiate regulatory change. The United States and Japan, among others, are also sensitive to global competition, and each wants to be the first country where autonomous vehicles are widely used. However, some industry observers (for example, Wenderoth 2018) predict that Baidu, a Chinese company, will capture the headlines as the first company to sell autonomous vehicles to its nation's travelers, rather than Waymo, GM, or Toyota. If so, the United States should be more concerned with the large welfare costs that residents have incurred because of unnecessary regulatory delays to autonomous-vehicle adoption than with the blow to its national pride.

Part 2

Potential Effects of Autonomous Vehicles

3

The Potential Effects of Autonomous Vehicles on Economic Sectors

Traditional automobiles produced enormous benefits to the United States when they were introduced in the early 1900s. They improved travelers' accessibility for existing trips, which had been taken by horse or railroad, and facilitated new trips. Automobiles also dramatically changed land use because people could live in roomier and less expensive houses on larger lots, at some distance from their workplaces. While automobiles displaced some existing jobs and reduced the use of other modes of transportation, they also created new jobs, especially in car production and servicing and in building and maintaining the U.S. road system. However, as the country continued to grow and automobiles were used more frequently for work and nonwork trips, the social costs of automobiles increased, including congestion, fatal and nonfatal accidents, air pollution, and the adverse effects on travelers' emotional health.

The introduction of large trucks to carry freight improved industry efficiency and productivity, but it also contributed to motor vehicles' harmful effects on congestion, health, the environment, and safety. In addition, large trucks damaged road pavement and bridges and threatened the viability of freight railroads, which were hamstrung by economic regulations, as they captured a large share of freight traffic, especially in high-value commodities.

By enacting inefficient policies for the road infrastructure that was used by cars and trucks, policymakers failed to maximize the benefits and reduce the social costs of those modes of transportation. Autonomous vehicles can reduce the welfare costs created by inefficient public policies in an environment of nonautonomous vehicles. They have the potential to reduce congestion, improve health and safety, and increase mobility for those people who do not have access to or cannot drive a vehicle; improve land use in urban areas by freeing up parking space that could be used for more socially desirable purposes; and disrupt but have overall positive effects on the labor market and the U.S. transportation system. However, government policy could strongly affect the extent to which those benefits are realized.

From an economic perspective, autonomous vehicles' most important effect is likely to be on congestion, because transportation is an input of many other economic activities. The significant improvement in highway travel time and its reliability attributable to autonomous vehicles is likely to generate benefits beyond the transportation sector. Indeed, highway traffic is most dysfunctional in dense urban areas. Cities thrive by connecting people, and when urban mobility falters, cities lose their capacity to generate economic vitality, including employment, job growth, idea sharing, and innovation. When cities fail, national economies suffer, so it is not hyperbole to claim that problems generated by urban traffic congestion rise to the level of national importance and that autonomous vehicles may benefit an entire economy by ameliorating those problems.

By reducing congestion, reducing travel time, and improving travel-time reliability, the adoption of autonomous vehicles could also yield other significant economic benefits:

Employment benefits. Individuals' choices of employers and employers' choices of workers could expand and result in greater employment. Chetty and others (2014), for example, finds that longer commuting times are strongly and negatively related to the probability that a household will escape poverty, implying that reductions in congestion could expand job opportunities and increase employment, especially for the least affluent members of society.

Agglomeration benefits. Firms and urban residents benefit from the spatial concentration of economic activities, known as agglomeration economies (Glaeser and Gottlieb 2009). Puga (2010) summarizes the evidence that urban density contributes to agglomeration economies and higher earnings. Thus reductions in congestion and improved travel times may improve those economies because people in all walks of life could reach their destinations more quickly and thereby share information more easily, finish certain tasks sooner, and so on.

Trade benefits. Anderson and van Wincoop (2004) shows that travel distance and travel time represent important components of the cost of international trade, which accounts for some of the freight flows over the U.S. transportation network. Those factors are also an important cost of the freight flows generated by intracity and intercity trade. Truck transportation carries a large share of U.S. intracity, intercity, and international freight flows. Reductions in congestion on urban and intercity highways lower the cost of shipping goods and increase freight flows, resulting in more production and consumption throughout the U.S. economy.

Productivity benefits. Improving the speed and reliability of freight traffic enables firms to reduce their inventories and to improve productivity (Shirley and Winston 2004). Productivity is further enhanced if all inputs in a firm's production process can reach their destinations faster. For example, Prud'homme and Lee (1999) estimates that a region's productivity increases 1.3 percent when the area that can be reached in a given time period increases by 10 percent. Thus reductions in congestion can broadly affect an entire economy's productivity.

How big an impact could autonomous vehicles have on the economy? No one can know for certain at this early stage. However, our calculations suggest that the economic benefits could be quite substantial and that they are likely to be broadly consistent with the impact of other significant improvements in mobility in the United States.

In the next three chapters, we report on an econometric model developed to estimate the causal effects of highway congestion on the growth rates of gross domestic product (GDP), employment, wages, and commodity-freight flows for congested counties in California. Lacking a natural experiment to measure congestion's effects, we use a plausible instrumental variable for congestion that reflects exogenous political considerations in highway spending, and we perform several tests that indicate that our estimates are not likely to be biased by omitted variables or reverse causality. Our estimation results for California are corroborated by findings in the literature on the effects of reducing congestion in specific sectors and by circumstantial evidence on the effects of reducing congestion in nontransport sectors. We then use the econometric estimates to simulate how widespread adoption of autonomous vehicles would impact the economic performance measures by reducing congestion levels in California. Finally, we extrapolate those findings to the nation by presenting a base-case and more-conservative estimates for sensitivity analysis.

We summarize our main findings here so nontechnical readers may pass over the technical chapters and skip to chapter 7, which discusses other effects of autonomous vehicles in a nontechnical manner. To predict the effects of autonomous vehicles on the California economy, we assume that autonomous vehicles would lead to a 50 percent reduction in freeway delays (see chapter 6 for details). Strikingly, we estimate that if California motorists had been using self-driving vehicles in 2010, the state would have created nearly 350,000 additional jobs that year, increased its real GDP by $35 billion, and raised workers' earnings by nearly $15 billion.[1] Using available 2007 data on freight flows between California counties as a measure of trade benefits, we find that autonomous vehicles would have increased the value of intercounty shipments of commodities by $57 billion.

Extrapolating those effects to the nation, we predict that autonomous vehicles in 2010 would have added 3 million additional jobs to the U.S. economy, raised the nation's annual growth rate by 1.8 percentage points from a 2010 baseline GDP of about $14.6 trillion, and increased annual labor earnings by more than $100 billion. In other words, the economic benefits to the United States are nearly eight times greater than those to California.

Naturally, an intuitive back-of-the envelope calculation of the potential economy-wide benefits that autonomous vehicles could generate by reducing congestion would be helpful. However, this type of calculation is difficult here because we are estimating benefits in nontransport sectors, where the benefits depend in a complex way on how consumers and firms respond to travel-time savings from reduced congestion by adjusting labor supply, production, and the like to reach new equilibrium levels of wages, employment, trade flows, and GDP growth.

Intuitively, it is well known that a given reduction in travel costs generally increases the value of a transportation network and the social gains that it generates by manyfold because the cost savings exponentially increase accessibility to more parts (nodes) of the network. Thus although our estimates may seem implausibly large, the significant improvements in mobility attributable to autonomous-vehicle use positively affect a considerable quantity of the nation's inputs (labor and capital) and outputs that are transported on the extensive integrated network of local, state, and federal roads.[2] Sensitivity analysis also indicates that even if very conservative assumptions are made about the effects of autonomous vehicles on reducing congestion, such as they are 50 percent lower for the United States as a whole than they are for California, then autonomous vehicles would still generate significant improvements in the nation's annual rate of growth that approach 1 percentage point.

In sum, substantial reductions in congestion and improvements in travel time and travel-time reliability for automobiles and trucks have the potential to generate macroeconomic (supply-side) stimulative effects because more efficient transportation can facilitate favorable improvements in the labor, urban, trade, and industrial sectors that result in more people working, shopping, trading, and producing goods. The additional employment and better job-matching attributable to faster and more reliable commutes, the increased freight flows attributable to the reduction in transport costs, and the higher productivity attributable to reduced transit time for both capital and labor could combine to significantly increase the U.S. growth rate. Moreover, the findings we summarize from our simulations to preview those effects account only for the economic effects of self-driving cars through reductions in congestion, and so almost certainly understate the benefits of autonomous vehicles. As explained in chapter 7, there are a myriad of other ways in which autonomous vehicles could improve social welfare.

4

Estimating the Effects of Congestion on Economic-Performance Measures

Only fragmentary evidence exists of the effects of congestion on an economy. For example, Hymel (2009), Sweet (2014), and Angel and Blei (2015) find that highway congestion is associated with slower job growth in U.S. metropolitan areas, while Light (2007) uses the Bureau of Labor Statistics' American Time-Use Survey to estimate reductions in workers' productivity and income that are caused by traffic delays from highway congestion. This chapter provides a more comprehensive empirical picture of the effects of highway congestion on the U.S. economy as a basis for estimating the potential benefits from autonomous vehicles' effect on congestion.

This picture reflects estimates of the causal effect of highway congestion on the growth rates of several different measures of economic performance. This empirical analysis focuses on California because the state has several highly congested urban areas, including eleven of the top sixteen highway bottlenecks in the nation (CPCS Transcom 2015), and its counties have had the option, since the early 1960s, to pass local sales taxes to fund spending for specific transportation projects that could reduce congestion.[1]

Such duly named "self-help" county taxes amount to a quasi-natural experiment because they have been enacted at various times by various counties primarily because public officials have successfully addressed various political issues, rather than seizing on economic factors relevant to economic growth. Keith Dunn, the executive director of California's Self-Help Counties Coalition, notes that for the past twenty years the passage of any proposed self-help tax legislation has required the support of at least 67 percent of eligible voters. Building such support requires skillful political leaders who are willing to conduct sufficient outreach and can craft legislation that embodies a successful compromise among several competing interests, independent of economic conditions in the county.[2] Accordingly, our identification strategy is to use the additional modest highway spending that is funded by self-help tax legislation as a valid instrument to determine the causal effect of highway congestion on measures of economic performance.

It could be argued that there must be some degree to which traffic conditions motivate efforts to raise a tax and motivate voters to support it. However, as discussed in detail below, self-help county taxes amount to a broad tax covering all travel modes and infrastructure, not just automobile transportation. In fact, roads get a modest share of the money—a share that must accumulate for decades before it generates reductions in congestion. Thus the causal path from road congestion to the passage of a self-help county tax that is expected to result in reasonably prompt reductions in congestion is far from clear a priori, and we find no evidence to suggest that such a path exists.

The Model

Traditional efficiency analyses of highway congestion measure the delay costs that motorists who travel during peak travel periods impose on other motorists.[3] This study goes beyond the external costs to other motorists by using panel data to estimate the effect that highway congestion has on the economic performance of urban areas in California, as measured by their GDP, employment, labor-earnings, and trade-flow growth rates.[4] The model begins with the demand for transportation, measured by traffic volume (V), and the supply of transportation, measured by infrastructure capacity (W). An equilibrium where transportation demand is sufficiently greater than transportation supply results in road congestion (C), so we adopt a formulation used by many authors, in which congestion rises as a power of the volume-capacity ratio:

$$C = f(V/W)^{\alpha}, \tag{4-1}$$

where α is a constant that, for example, takes on a value of 2.5 for urban arterials and 4.0 for urban expressways (Small, Winston, and Evans 1989).

Given the preceding conceptual discussion and following previous work, our general model is a reduced form that relates congestion, which tends to grow over time because capacity cannot keep up with traffic volume, to economic growth and other controls. It can be described as

$$G_{it} = f(C_{it}, X_{it}, \varepsilon_{it}), \tag{4-2}$$

where G_{it} is the growth rate of an economic performance variable in geographic unit i during year t, C_{it} is the level of congestion, X_{it} is an array of controls, and ε_{it} is a random error term.

In our empirical work, we use a log-linear specification, so our model can be summarized as

$$\ln G_{it} = \gamma \times \ln C_{it} + X_{it}\beta + \phi_t + c_i + \varepsilon_{it},$$

where γ is the causal effect of congestion level C on the growth rate, $X\beta$ is an array of controls and coefficients, ϕ_t is the year dummy, c_i is the urban-area dummy, and ε is the random error term.

Below, we summarize the available data to measure congestion and the growth-rate performance variables. We then describe and provide extensive justification for the instrument for congestion, discuss the data used to measure it, and summarize the final sample used for estimation.

Congestion

Congestion is measured using estimates of annual hours of delay per auto commuter from the Texas A&M Transportation Institute (TTI). Data are provided for the years 1982–2011 for all urban areas with more than 500,000 people. Auto commuters are defined as people who make trips by car during morning (6:00–10:00 a.m.) and evening (3:00–7:00 p.m.) peak periods. The numbers of auto commuters are estimated using data from the National Household Travel Survey, conducted by the Federal Highway Administration (FHWA). The Texas Transportation Institute adds measurements of peak-period delays to measurements of travel delay during nonpeak hours to estimate the total annual delay experienced by auto commuters.

To compute congestion-induced delays during both peak and nonpeak periods, TTI estimates two speeds for a given roadway segment: the free-flow speed, or the average speed observed during light traffic periods of the day (for example, 10:00 p.m. until 5:00 a.m. the next morning), and the actual speed observed during a given time interval of the day. By comparing actual and free-flow speeds, TTI is able to estimate congestion-induced speed reductions for different hours of the day. It then scales up those speed reductions using traffic-volume data to compute the total amount of time lost to traffic congestion.

In recent years, travel-speed data have come from INRIX, a private company that monitors travel times on most major roads in the United States. (The institute has made considerable efforts to align earlier data with INRIX data.) Traffic-volume data come from the FHWA's Highway Performance Monitoring System. The INRIX speed data are recorded in fifteen-minute intervals for every day of the year, allowing TTI to account for both daily and hourly variations in congestion levels.[5] For the sample of California urban areas from 1982 to 2011, discussed later, annual delay per auto commuter ranged from two hours to eighty-nine hours, with a mean delay of thirty-four hours per year.

Economic-Performance Measures

County-level economic performance measures are used that include real GDP, wages, employment, and originating freight traffic transported by truck. Real GDP, wages, and employment data for the period 1982–2011 were provided by the Brookings Institution's Metropolitan Policy Program, using data from Moody's Analytics.[6] Freight flows, measured as thousands of tons of commodities transported by truck across California counties, were obtained from the California Statewide Freight Forecasting Model, which combines 2007 data from the FHWA's Freight Analysis Framework with demographic data to forecast flows for 2010.[7] The forecast flows are not adjusted to account for any unanticipated changes in congestion.

GDP, wages, and employment are expressed in terms of annual growth rates as

$$Growth_t^{DV} = \ln \left(\frac{DV_{t+1}}{DV_t} \right) \qquad (4\text{-}3)$$

where $Growth_t^{DV}$ is the annual growth rate of a dependent-variable performance measure DV in year t, DV_{t+1} is the level of the dependent variable DV in year $t + 1$, and DV_t is the level of the dependent variable DV in year t.[8] Because we have commodity-flow data only for the years 2007 and 2010, we express the dependent variable for this performance measure as a three-year growth rate—the difference between 2010 and 2007 levels.

Using Self-Help County Taxes as an Instrument for Highway Congestion

There are two fundamental challenges to estimating the effect of congestion on an economic performance measure (for example, employment): omitted variables and reverse causality. Omitted variables most likely arise because some variables that affect both congestion and an economic performance measure, such as certain types of weather (Sweet 2014), are omitted from the model because they are difficult to quantify. Reverse causality most likely occurs because an economic performance measure is closely related to the volume of passenger and freight traffic on the road and thus will affect congestion. The standard approach to minimizing the bias from omitted variables and reverse causality is to use an appropriate instrumental variable that is correlated with the explanatory variable of interest (in this case, highway congestion) but is not correlated with the dependent variable (for example, employment) or with omitted variables that affect the dependent variable.

Given that congestion is a function of the volume-capacity ratio, we argue that self-help taxes represent a valid instrument because they are correlated with congestion by improving existing capacity (W) on certain roads, but the revenue that they raise is too modest to directly affect economic activity (G) and traffic volume (V), which would cause two-way causality. Furthermore, because passage of the tax legislation is largely determined by political factors, it is unlikely that there are omitted variables that affect the performance variables and that are also correlated with self-help taxes. In what follows, we justify our choice of an appropriate instrument by providing a brief overview of self-help transportation taxes and explaining how we specify and measure our instrument; discussing how the taxes are influenced by politics; explaining why the taxes are exogenous to the performance measures; and arguing why our estimates of the effect of highway congestion on the performance variables are likely to represent a lower bound.

An Overview of Self-Help County Taxes and Measurement of the Instrument

The early California legislation enabling a county self-help tax to fund transportation projects was intended, among other things, to help reduce highway congestion.[9] Counties used part of this additional tax revenue to improve existing highway capacity by performing repairs to upgrade the condition of certain roads, maintaining the pavement to a higher standard, and, in some cases, building modest connectors between roads and perhaps rehabilitating a lane. The funds, however, were not used to build new freeway capacity. In addition, any highway project was subject to the federal government and California permitting and environmental standards, which meant that considerable time and effort would have to be spent to satisfy those standards before actual physical work on California roads could begin.[10]

Data on self-help county taxes were collected from the website of each of the California counties in our analysis sample and from an initial summary by Crabbe and others (2005).[11] Counties vary by the years during which they voted on and either passed or renewed a transportation sales tax, the sales tax rate, and the share of the transportation tax revenue dedicated to highways. Table 4-1 shows the factors that contribute to the variation in California counties' accumulation of highway tax revenue over time by listing the preceding information for the counties with measurable congestion that passed transportation sales taxes.[12] The share of self-help revenue going to highway projects varies noticeably, ranging from 0 percent (in fourteen of the forty times that counties could have allocated revenue to highways) to 100 percent (in Santa Clara County, 1984).

Self-help ballot measures come with specific expenditure plans detailing how revenue from the taxes will be spent. Because the self-help taxes themselves are small and because only a fraction of the tax revenues are dedicated to highways, it can take considerable time for a county's self-help tax to raise the funds for the more expensive highway projects that are intended to reduce congestion. Thus we express our instrument for congestion in county i at time t as the cumulative share of the county sales tax base that is spent on self-help highway projects, $cumulativeHighwayShare_{it}$, which is expressed as

$$cumulativeHighwayShare_{it} = \Sigma_{j=1982}^{t}\, taxRate_{ij} \times \%highway_{ij}, \quad (4\text{-}4)$$

where $taxRate_{ij}$ is the local transportation tax rate for county i in year j (for example, 0.50 or 0.25 percent)[13] and $\%highway_{ij}$ is the share of the county's self-help tax revenue that is allocated to highway proj-

Table 4-1

California Local Transportation Sales Tax, by County and Year, 1969–2008 (units as indicated)

County	Tax proposal on ballot (year)	Tax proposal passed or renewed (year)	Tax rate (percent)	Share of tax dedicated to highways (percent)
Alameda	1969, 1986, 1998, 2000	1969, 1986, 2000	0.5	0, 43, 17
Contra Costa	1969, 1986, 1988, 2004	1969, 1988, 2004	0.5	0, 37, 19
Fresno	1986, 2002, 2006	1986, 2006	0.5	74, 29
Los Angeles	1980, 1990, 2008	1980, 1990, 2008	0.5	0, 0, 20
Madera	1990, 2002, 2006	1990, 2006	0.5	0, 51
Marin	1969, 1990, 1998, 2004, 2006	1969, 2004	0.5	0, 8
Orange	1984, 1989, 1990, 2006	1990, 2006	0.5	43, 43
Riverside	1988, 2002	1988, 2002	0.5	51, 43
Sacramento	1988, 2004	1988, 2004	0.5	63, 12
San Bernardino	1987, 1989, 2004	1989, 2004	0.5	53, 37
San Diego	1987, 2004	1987, 2004	0.5	33, 33
San Francisco	1969, 1989, 2003	1969, 1989, 2003	0.5	0, 0, 0
San Joaquin	1990, 2006	1990, 2006	0.5	25, 20
San Mateo	1969, 1974, 1988, 2004	1969, 1974, 1988, 1996, 2000, 2008	0.5	0, 0, 29, 28
Santa Clara	1976, 1984, 1992, 1996, 2000, 2008	1976, 1984, 1996, 2000, 2008	0.5	0, 100, 31, 31, 0
Santa Cruz	1978, 2004	1978	0.5	0

ects in year *j*, as stipulated by the expenditure plan developed by county *i*. Additional reasons for using a cumulative measure are discussed below.

In short, we refer to this construct as the cumulative share of the self-help tax base dedicated to highways. Consider, for example, Fresno County. In 1986 Fresno began imposing a 0.5 percent transportation sales tax, 74 percent of which went to highway projects. Thus 0.37 percent of the county's sales tax base went to self-help highway projects in 1986. An additional 0.37 percent did so in 1987, meaning that 0.74 percent of the cumulative tax base since 1982 (the starting year of our sample) had gone to highways. In other words,

$$cumulativeHighwayShare_{Fresno, 1985} = 0\%,$$
$$cumulativeHighwayShare_{Fresno, 1986} = 0.37\%,$$
$$cumulativeHighwayShare_{Fresno, 1987} = 0.74\%,$$

and so forth.

Alternative ways of specifying this instrument are discussed later, but we stress here that the actual dollar amount of highway revenues from self-help taxes is not used as an instrument because dollar amounts are a function of the size of the economy, which is endogenous.[14]

Because expenditure plans may change when counties vote to renew a self-help tax, $taxRate_{ij}$ and $\%highway_{ij}$ may vary across years.[15] In the years preceding the enactment of a self-help tax measure and in the years following the discontinuation of a self-help tax measure, $taxRate_{ij}$ and $highway_{ij}$ are set to 0.

By using a cumulative measure of the share of the local sales tax base going to self-help highway projects, we are able to account for lags between revenue intake and transportation expenditures, differences in the rate at which counties accumulate self-help funds, and the modest amount of revenue for highway projects that a county can accumulate each year from a self-help tax (for example, in 2014 the majority of counties received less than $100 million in self-help tax revenue [California Department of Transportation 2014]), compared with the high cost of certain highway projects, which could be as much as hundreds of millions of dollars over many years. Again, self-help taxes are not passed with the expectation that they will raise substantial revenues capable of funding multibillion-dollar highway projects that will add significant new capacity.

Political Considerations

Gasoline-tax revenues have been influenced by political forces at all levels of government. The federal gasoline tax, which supports the FHWA's Highway Trust Fund, which pays for road maintenance and improvements (Langer, Maheshri, and Winston 2017), has been held hostage to an ideological battle in which increases are supported by moderates but opposed by both fiscal conservatives, who do not want to increase taxes, and social progressives, who believe the tax is regressive and instead encourage travelers to use transit and non-motorized forms of transportation. Thus the tax has remained at $0.18 cents per gallon since 1993 throughout periods of strong economic growth and recessions and during a period in which President Obama, a Democrat, had majorities in both houses of Congress. The Highway Trust Fund now runs a deficit.

In contrast to Congress, nearly twenty states have been able to reach a political compromise to gain enough support to raise their gasoline tax. For example, in 2016 the California gasoline tax was the fifth highest in the nation. Nonetheless, public transit, environmental groups who support biking and walking trails, and other interests were part of the coalition that banded together in 2017 to support a significant $0.12 per gallon increase in the California gasoline tax in return for a notable share of the funds. In 2018 California voters defeated a proposition that would have rescinded the gas-tax increase. Li, Linn, and Muehlegger (2014) discusses the evidence on political considerations that affect state gasoline taxes.

In contrast to changes in federal and state gasoline taxes, self-help taxes must be explicitly approved by at least two-thirds of a county's voters. Thus passing such tax legislation is strongly determined by political considerations—namely, whether a political leader is willing to expend the necessary resources, especially time, to conduct a broad outreach that will successfully bring several coalitions together to support additional spending on various transportation projects, including but not limited to highway projects. Of course, it is reasonable to assume that political leaders are motivated to introduce a self-help tax because they believe its effects on a county's transportation system would help them politically. We are not aware of empirical evidence of the political benefits of self-help taxes in California, but Huet-Vaughn (2019) finds that spending on road and bridge projects in New Jersey as part of the American Recovery and Reinvestment Act of 2009 increased Democratic presidential and Senate vote shares in municipalities near the projects.[16]

The political challenge to gain two-thirds of the county's votes to pass self-help tax legislation is formidable and works to marginalize economic considerations. For example, Sacramento County proposed a self-help tax in 2016, and its supporters made a concerted effort to gain voter approval. But the tax was voted down in November even though 65 percent of the voters favored it (narrowly missing the supermajority mark). Retrospective assessments identified several problems: the ballot was very long, which discouraged some potentially supportive voters from actually voting on the transportation tax measure; supporters of transit were dissatisfied with transit's share of the funds and wanted a greater share; and opponents of transit thought transit's share of the funds was too large and wanted it to be cut.[17] If political leaders put a self-help tax before Sacramento voters in future elections, they will have to focus more intently on building a successful coalition to gain approval.

Sacramento's experience is not unusual. Many California counties failed to pass a self-help transportation tax on their first try but eventually passed one, regardless of the economic conditions at the time, because they were more successful at mobilizing political support. Some of the variation in voting outcomes on self-help initiatives is clearly a result of a California Supreme Court ruling in the mid-1990s that raised the voting threshold for self-help tax measures from 50 percent to 67 percent. Arguably, a county that passed a self-help measure with 55 percent of the vote in the 1980s showed the same public commitment to the tax as a county that failed to pass a self-help measure with 55 percent of the vote in the late 1990s; the only difference between the two outcomes is the higher voting threshold, which is clearly exogenous.

Crabbe and others (2005) similarly suggests that California's expenditure plans for self-help tax revenue were designed primarily with political and technical considerations in mind. For example, because ballot measures must specify the intended uses of the tax revenue, expenditure plans are crafted to appeal to a variety of different interest groups. One might also raise concerns that the expenditure plans are not reflective of how the sales-tax revenue is actually spent—that is, that the county transportation authorities responsible for managing new projects do not adhere strictly to the expenditure plan that was crafted to gain political support and instead alter the plan for their own purposes. However, it appears that most self-help tax measures provide little flexibility for technocrat discretion. Crabbe and others (2005) notes that most local transportation tax measures commit a large proportion of their revenue for specific projects, limiting the power of transportation authorities to reallocate revenue once the tax is approved.

Finally, the prioritization of projects that are to be funded by self-help taxes appears to be shaped by considerations that are independent of performance measures of the economy. In particular, Crabbe and others (2005) observes that the most common project-prioritization criteria are ensuring that sales-tax revenue is distributed fairly across all geographic subregions in a county; satisfying established growth-management requirements for new development projects; and, if possible, leveraging state and federal sources of funding. Thus in all such cases, bureaucratic and political constraints appear to be shaping the order in which transportation projects that are funded by county self-help tax revenue are implemented.

Exogeneity of Self-Help Taxes

Why do the self-help taxes not lead to bias from reverse causality or omitted variables? Reverse causality would exist if the revenue expenditures increased economic activity in other ways besides by improving existing road capacity and reducing congestion. As indicated in the tax-competition literature (for example, Agrawal 2015), local sales taxes can affect employment and other measures of performance. But those taxes are much greater than the self-help taxes considered here. For example, Rohlin and Thompson (2018) finds that an increase of 1.0 percentage point in the combined local and state sales tax rate results in a modest 0.2 to 0.3 reduction in the share of total employment in a county pair. But given that the actual level of California self-help taxes is only 0.5 percent, the direct impact on economic performance would be quite small.[18] In comparison, the discussion in chapter 3 indicates that the effect of congestion on the economic performance measures is likely to be considerably larger.

Similarly, self-help taxes do not directly affect the performance measures by affecting traffic volume. Downs' law (Downs 1962) states that peak-hour congestion rises to meet maximum expressway capacity because of latent demand, suggesting that travelers who used less preferred routes, modes, and times of day would shift to the newly constructed or significantly expanded highway. But, as noted, self-help taxes are not used to build new California freeways, which would affect traffic volume. Instead, they are used for modest improvements in the existing capacity of local and state roads, which would not induce much traffic, especially because congestion on major freeways would persist and discourage any behavioral changes in latent demand.[19]

We performed a suggestive statistical test of the effect of a self-help tax on measures of economic performance. We constructed a dummy variable that indicates whether a county's voters have approved self-help tax legislation in a given year. We then estimated separate regressions of the effect of the dummy variable on real GDP and employment (in levels and growth rates) for the sample counties and time period, controlling for county fixed effects and congestion delays because by reducing the latter, self-help taxes could affect a county's economic performance. We explored specifications that included as many as ten lags and two leads for the self-help-tax dummy variable, and we consistently find that its effect on both GDP and employment was small and statistically insignificant, indicating that self-help taxes do not have a direct effect on a county's economic performance. We show later that the cumulative expenditure share of self-help taxes does affect congestion delays.

Omitted variables may create bias if they are correlated with the specific components of the instrument. But the exogeneity of $taxRate_{ij}$ is self-evident because there is almost no variation in $taxRate_{ij}$ across either time or counties. More specifically, every county has a self-help tax of 0.5 percent, except for Sonoma, which has a rate of 0.25 percent and is not included in TTI's sample of the most congested urban areas in the country.[20]

Among those counties in the study that eventually passed a self-help tax measure, we argue that both the year in which the tax was enacted and the share of tax revenue dedicated to highway projects are exogenous to economic trends and conditions in the county. Several pieces of evidence support this claim.

First, the sample of California urban areas includes only those that are in TTI's sample of the most congested urban areas in the United States from 1982 to 2011. Thus those areas experienced congestion throughout the period covered by the sample, and they were not subjected to an economic shock that caused their residents to suddenly become concerned about congestion and to enthusiastically support additional taxes to reduce it.

Second, it is possible that either the timing of passage of a self-help tax or the share dedicated to highway projects is driven by earlier economic or congestion trends. For example, if a county observed that congestion levels were rising rapidly, that county might have been more likely to pass a self-help tax or to dedicate a larger share of self-help tax revenue to highway projects. In other words, in the sample, policymakers may have been responding to historic trends in congestion when making self-help tax decisions.

We test whether a hypothetical correlation between voter approval of self-help taxes and within-county congestion trends exists by computing the congestion growth rate for the year before the passage of an urban area's first self-help tax.[21] Because there are only ten California urban areas in this final sample, we simply mapped this measure of annual congestion growth rates before passage of the self-help tax onto the share of an urban area's sales tax base going to highway projects (that is, our self-help tax instrument) and the year in which the urban area first passed a self-help tax. Neither the share of revenue going to self-help highway projects (figure 4-1a) nor the timing of the passage of a self-help tax (figure 4-1b) appears to correlate with congestion trends preceding the enactment of a self-help measure. Similar findings were obtained when we considered annual GDP or growth rates instead of congestion for the year before the passage of the first self-help tax. We also find no correlation between the share of the self-help tax base going to highways and the level of congestion or the level of GDP that an urban area experienced during the year in which it passed its self-help tax measure. If underlying economic or congestion considerations motivated the allocation of self-help funds to highways, we would expect such a correlation to exist.

We provide additional empirical evidence by specifying a county's voters' decision to pass self-help tax legislation as a dummy variable and estimating a binary logit model to determine whether economic variables, including real GDP, employment, and congestion delays, affected the outcome of the proposed tax legislation. Because the economic variables were correlated, we estimated separate models of

Figure 4-1a
**Correlation between Proposed Share of Self-Help Tax
Expenditures on Highway Projects and Congestion Growth
in Year Preceding Passage of First Self-Help Tax**

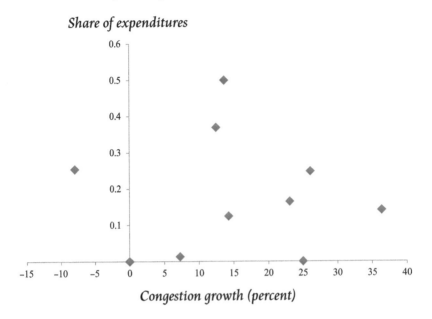

Share of expenditures

Congestion growth (percent)

Figure 4-1b
**Correlation between Passage of First Self-Help Tax and
Congestion Growth in Year Preceding Passage**

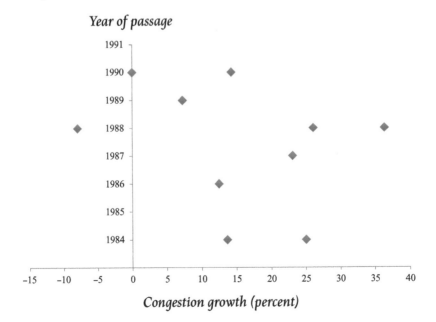

Year of passage

Congestion growth (percent)

each variable's effect (in levels and growth rates), including as many as five lags for each variable as well as county fixed effects. We find that the estimated coefficients of the economic variables were generally small and had statistically insignificant effects on voters' approval of a self-help county tax, which again suggests that support for those taxes is determined by political not economic factors.

It would be desirable to quantify some relevant political variables and to assess their effects on voters' approval of a self-help county tax. However, our discussions with knowledgeable individuals on the matter indicated that the key political variables included the formation of transparent proposed expenditures, accountability that the proposed expenditures would be enacted, and political "entrepreneurship" and resources, especially time spent by political leaders and their associates engaging with the community to craft legislation and to generate a large voter turnout to gain passage. Generally, self-help county legislation that is passed reflects the efforts of hundreds of people and not simply those of a single individual who may be successful at getting legislation enacted. Consequently, it is difficult to quantify and test potential political variables that would help to explain the passage of specific self-help tax legislation that is proposed.

Finally, because economic outcomes, congestion, and cumulative self-help tax expenditures may have a common time trend at the local (county) level, owing to, for example, a natural disaster, such as an earthquake, that may affect only certain counties in California, we conducted a sensitivity analysis (discussed in detail later) by estimating our growth models with random time-trend effects. (Note that these differ from random effects.) We find that controlling for those effects did not materially affect the parameter estimates.

Bounding the Potential Bias Caused
by Omitted Variables

Our findings will indicate that, compared with the instrumental variables (IV) estimates, the ordinary least squares estimates of the effect of congestion on the performance measures are biased downward. If that is the true bias of the ordinary least squares (OLS) estimates, then it is plausible that the IV estimates are informative as, at least, lower-bound estimates of the effects of congestion on the performance measures. However, before providing that interpretation of the IV estimates, it is important to consider whether there are omitted variables that would cause the true bias of the OLS estimates to be biased upward instead of downward. That is, what omitted variables are either negatively related to congestion and have a positive effect on the performance variables or positively related to congestion and have a negative effect on the performance variables? We identify such variables, and we conduct additional estimations, which show that our initial findings that the OLS estimates are biased downward are robust.

In sum, we argue that, in contrast to conventional models in public finance, the revenue raised by self-help taxes for highway projects is not the result of welfare-maximizing decisions by policymakers subject to current economic conditions. Instead, it is determined primarily by the effectiveness of county leaders and their associates at mobilizing the political support of a supermajority of diverse coalitions of voters, which bears little relation to a county's current economic conditions and justifies our use of the self-help taxes as a valid instrument for highway congestion in an empirical analysis. We have strengthened the justification by explaining why the self-help county taxes affect only congestion, do not directly affect the performance variables and traffic volume, and are unlikely to be related to the omitted variables.

Constructing a Consistent Unit of Analysis and the Final Sample

The TTI data on average annual hours of delay per auto commuter are measured at the urban-area level. Data on urban-area economic characteristics, however, are sparse. Thus Hymel (2009) and Sweet (2014), for example, rely on data for metropolitan statistical areas (MSAs) to construct dependent variables that proxy for urban-area-level economic conditions. It is not feasible for us to use MSA-level data here because the allocation of self-help tax funds is decided at the county level, not the MSA level. This means that a county must be the unit of analysis for our instrumental variable—the cumulative share of sales revenue dedicated to self-help highway projects. In addition, we must rely on county-level data to construct commodity flows and GDP.[22]

We therefore use county-level data to measure the dependent and instrumental variables but then transform those county-level measures into urban-area measures to align them with the congestion variable. Specifically, we apply the following transformation:

$$X_j = \Sigma_{i=1}^{N_j} X_i \times P_{ij}, \qquad (4\text{-}5)$$

where X_j is the measure of variable X for urban area j, X_i is the measure of variable X for county i, P_{ij} is the share of urban area j's population that lived in county i in 2010, as indicated by the U.S. census, and N_j is the number of counties that overlap with urban area j.[23] Thus in all models using annual growth rates for GDP, employment, and wages, the unit of analysis is the urban area.

Using the Bureau of Economic Analysis MSA-level data on employment and earnings for the 1982–2011 time period, we perform robustness checks on whether the results of the jobs- and labor-earnings growth models hold when we construct the dependent variable using MSA-level, as opposed to county-level, growth rates. As noted later, we find that our results are robust to this alternative specification, suggesting that our estimates of the effect of highway congestion on employment and earnings are not driven by our reliance on county-level data.

We include freight flows across California counties only because our instrument for congestion is valid only for California counties that had already voted for a self-help tax during the period studied. The implication of this restriction is that we understate the effect of congestion on freight flows because we do not include its effect on flows between California counties and U.S. urban areas outside California or between California counties and foreign urban areas.[24] The appendix describes the computation performed to measure freight flows across urban areas.

Given an urban area as the basic unit of observation, we define the estimation sample to consist of all urban areas that (1) have measurable annual congestion reported in the TTI database and (2) overlap with counties that had passed a countywide self-help tax by 2011. We further limit the sample to (3) the years in which at least one of an urban area's counties voted on (or had previously voted on) a countywide transportation sales tax.[25] We use the second and third restrictions to make the sample of counties more homogenous, specifically with respect to a county's political interest in pursuing and enacting a self-help tax. In particular, the third restriction ensures that we consider only the years in which an urban area has a serious interest in passing a self-help tax. Similarly, the second restriction ensures that the urban areas in the sample all possess the political will necessary to (eventually) implement a self-help tax. As a result, variation in our self-help tax measure reflects only two factors: the timing between the first self-help vote and the first successful self-help vote and the allocation of self-help funds to highway projects. As we have argued, both factors are driven primarily by political considerations.

Because TTI provides panel data on twelve urban areas in California for the 1982–2011 period, the sample initially consisted of 360 urban-area years. Given the aforementioned restrictions and one additional adjustment, we proceed with an unbalanced panel data set consisting of 256 observations.[26]

The sample used to estimate the effect of congestion on commodity flows consists of 100 observations because we have ten urban areas in the sample and estimates of commodity flows for each possible origin-destination pair (for example, there is a commodity flow to and from the Fresno urban area; there is also a commodity flow from Fresno to Riverside and from Riverside to Fresno).

Table 4-2 presents summary statistics for the variables used in the GDP, employment, and labor earnings and the commodity-flow models. The top panel shows that the California urban areas grew at a healthy rate during the sample period, although those areas also experienced contractionary periods. The bottom panel shows the effects of the Great Recession, as the urban-area commodity-flow growth rate declined, on average, during the period 2007–2010. In both models, the cumulative percentage of the sales tax base allocated to self-help highway projects for the urban areas in the sample, which is affected by when an urban area first voted on a self-help tax, is small—less than 9 percent.[27]

Table 4-2

Summary Statistics (percent, except as indicated)

GDP, employment, and labor earnings model	Average	Minimum	Maximum
Annual growth rate[a]			
Urban-area GDP	5.6	−9.3	18.0
Urban-area employment	1.3	−9.8	6.8
Urban-area labor earnings	5.3	−14.7	30.9
Annual delay per automobile commuter (hours)[b]	34.0	2.0	89.0
Annual sales-tax base allocated to self-help highway projects (percent)[c]	0.2	0.0	0.5
Cumulative sales-tax base allocated to self-help highway projects (percent)[c]	2.3	0.0	8.4
Urban-area population (in 1,000s)[b]	2,628	175	13,124
Commodity-flow model			
Three-year interurban-area commodity-flow growth rate (2007–2010)[d]	−36	−61	73
Annual delay per automobile commuter in 2007 (hours)[b]	41.4	14.0	86.0
Cumulative sales-tax base allocated to self-help highway projects in 2007 (percent)[c]	3.9	0.0	7.9
Urban-area population in 2007 (in 1,000s)[b]	2,729	390	12,800

a. Brookings Institution Metropolitan Policy Program and Moody's Analytics.

b. Texas Transportation Institute.

c. California County's websites and Crabbe and others (2005).

d. California Statewide Freight Forecasting Model.

5

Estimation Results Obtained from the Congestion Model

Three important considerations affect how we specify the effect of self-help taxes on congestion in the first-stage estimation. First, it may take considerable time for a county's self-help tax to raise the funds necessary to complete a project, especially because political compromises among competing interests and across geographical areas make it highly unlikely at any given time that the optimal level of funds has been raised and allocated to roads. Second, before they can begin actual roadwork, self-help counties must perform engineering analyses and obtain permits indicating that they have satisfied National Environment and Policy Act and California Environmental Quality Act reviews to ensure that projects are built in a safe and responsible manner and that they will not have adverse impacts on the environment and communities. Third, when counties begin roadwork, they may have to form work zones. A work zone is an area of a road where construction, maintenance, or utility-work activities occur, and it is typically marked by signs (especially ones that indicate reduced speed limits), traffic-channeling devices, barriers, and work vehicles.

Those considerations suggest that the initial expenditures of self-help tax funds on a project are unlikely to reduce congestion—and some are likely to be associated with increases of it[1]—and that it may take considerable time for counties to accumulate sufficient funds and to make sufficient progress to reduce congestion. Thus we specify a linear term to capture the initial effects of cumulative self-help highway spending on annual delay and a squared term to capture longer-term effects. Although this specification is not standard for instrumental variables, Sweet (2014) uses the same functional form in its instrumental-variables analysis of congestion, and it is a plausible characterization of the effect of self-help highway spending as it and the projects that it funds evolve and eventually reduce congestion.[2]

Table 5-1 presents first-stage estimation results that use our cumulative self-help tax instrument, total urban-area population, and urban-area and year fixed effects to predict the logged annual hours of delay per commuter. In alternative specifications described below, we include interactions between urban-area and time dummies to capture long-term, location-specific structural changes in the economy, such as shifts in an urban area's demographics or increases in the share of its urban population.[3]

The estimates of both cumulative self-help tax coefficients are statistically significant, and their signs are consistent with a plausible evolution of the effects of self-help highway expenditures. The positive coefficient for the linear term suggests that additional self-help tax revenue is associated with greater delay in the short run, as would be expected when work zones are formed at the beginning of a project. The negative coefficient for the squared term suggests that additional self-help tax revenue is associated with less delay in the long run as projects are completed, thereby increasing existing road capacity and improving road quality to facilitate higher speeds.[4]

It is useful to provide more perspective on those results. Using the estimated coefficients, we find that congestion levels begin to fall once the cumulative share of the local sales-tax base that is spent on self-help highway projects is roughly 7 percent.[5] The time it takes

Table 5-1
Model of Logged Annual Hours of Delay per Automobile Commuter

	Coefficient (Robust standard error)
Cumulative self-help-tax measure	0.257**
	(0.087)
Cumulative self-help-tax measure squared	−0.018**
	(0.008)
Total population	0.0001*
	(0.00007)
Urban-area fixed effects	Yes
Year fixed effects	Yes
Estimation sample	Years since first self-help vote, positive congestion
Sample size	256
Adjusted R^2	0.93
F statistic	4.82**

$^*p < 0.1$; $^{**}p < 0.05$; $^{***}p < 0.01$

Note: Robust standard errors account for clustering at the urban-area level of an unbalanced panel.

a county to reach that cumulative share depends on the share of the tax base that a county dedicates to self-help-tax highway projects each year. For example, if a county has an annual self-help tax of 0.5 percent and dedicates 100 percent of that tax to highway projects, holding all else constant, congestion levels for the county would start decreasing fourteen years after passing the self-help tax (6.99% / [0.50% × 1.00]). Put differently, for the first fourteen years, all other things being equal, more self-help highway expenditures cause more congestion; after fourteen years, more expenditures reduce congestion levels. As noted, depending on the project, some expenditures may pay for engineering analyses and the permitting process, which can take several years, or for maintenance and construction in work zones, which typically cause congestion delays.

For the average county in our sample, the share of the annual self-help tax dedicated to self-help highway projects is much less than 100 percent—roughly 34 percent;[6] thus because the rate of revenue accumulation is so slow, it takes roughly forty years for congestion levels to decline. In other words, only a minority of counties in our sample accumulated self-help highway revenue fast enough to cause congestion levels to fall in less than a few decades.

This finding is not particularly surprising because the political and institutional influences on raising and spending self-help highway tax revenues are likely to create significant inefficiencies. Winston and Langer (2006) finds that the effect of federal highway spending on reducing congestion delays was significantly compromised because funds were not allocated across and within states to minimize the cost of congestion delays; doing so would have reduced those costs by 40 percent. Because self-help county highway spending is so much less than federal-government highway spending, the inefficiencies and constraints on that spending may significantly increase the time it takes it to reduce congestion.

Accordingly, our discussion should be qualified because we have isolated the effect of self-help revenue when it may be combined with state and federal funds for certain larger projects that have a more immediate effect on reducing congestion. Thus an alternative—and possibly more accurate—explanation for the inverse-U relation between congestion and self-help expenditures is that what matters for congestion relief is the amount of self-help spending on highways, not the length of time since a self-help tax measure was passed. For example, suppose that a county spends only small amounts of its self-help tax revenue on small highway-improvement projects, such as repainting roads to identify a shoulder that is reserved for the use of bicyclists. Those marginal highway projects would probably increase congestion when they were being implemented because lanes might need to be shut down. However, we would not expect small projects on their own to have sizable long-run congestion-reducing effects. Thus if a county spent money on small projects for decades, we might expect cumulative revenue spending to be positively associated with highway congestion. In other words, small highway projects have all the negative side effects of increasing congestion in the short run and have few positive side effects of reducing congestion in the long run. At the same time, such projects could be pursued because they also have safety, environmental, and other benefits.

In contrast, more expensive highway projects, such as adding a lane, may raise congestion levels in the short run but reduce congestion in the long run.[7] But those projects are likely to be funded only if county self-help tax revenue is combined with greater funding from the state and federal governments. For example, Sacramento County's list of proposed projects in its 2016 proposed self-help tax legislation included a $700 million plan to add a lane to a freeway from midtown to its junction with another freeway, but the project could proceed only if the county's self-help tax revenues were supplemented with state and federal funds. Thus according to this interpretation of our findings, when counties spend their self-help tax revenue on projects that also receive state and federal funding, they experience more immediate reductions in congestion. When counties spend money on lots of small projects, they do not achieve immediate reductions in congestion; in fact, they may increase congestion levels for extended periods.

Because we were unable to collect data for each year of our sample on each county's self-help tax revenue expenditures for specific transportation projects, it is difficult for us to determine whether our findings reflect the effect of the passage of time or instead result from the types of projects that the counties chose to fund over time. Although we explored alternative specifications that might capture those considerations more fully than the preceding model did, we did not find that any of them led to a better understanding of how county self-help taxes affected congestion.[8] In sum, the first-stage estimation results indicate that the economic effects of our instrument are plausible and that the instrument is strongly correlated with congestion.[9]

Congestion's Effects on Economic Performance Measures

We use the first-stage estimates to instrument annual delay and estimate its causal effect on the economic-performance measures. We specify log-linear functional forms for each specification to present elasticities, and we control for both urban-area and year fixed effects, as well as for a time-varying measure of urban-area population size. Although there is some concern that populations may migrate in response to urban-area factors that affect both economic performance and congestion levels, we suspect that such correlations are small, especially net of the urban-area and year fixed effects. This hypothesis is supported by the fact that we do not find that the estimated congestion effects change noticeably when we exclude population size from the model.[10]

Table 5-2 presents ordinary least squares (OLS) and two-stage least squares (2SLS) estimates and shows the importance of controlling for the endogeneity of congestion. The OLS estimates of the effect of annual delays on the annual growth in jobs, GDP, and wages are generally much smaller and less statistically reliable than the corresponding 2SLS estimates. The 2SLS estimates indicate that a 10 percent reduction in congestion in a California urban area has a measurable effect on the performance measures, as both job and GDP growth increase by roughly 0.25 percent and wage growth increases by approximately 0.18 percent.[11] The quantitative responses are consistent with previous estimates of the effect of congestion on employment (Hymel 2009) and earnings (Light 2007).

In addition, the estimates are consistent with circumstantial evidence that suggests that workers attach a high cost to congestion that

Table 5-2
Effects of Congestion on the Economy

	Logged job growth		Logged GDP growth		Logged wage growth	
	OLS	2SLS	OLS	2SLS	OLS	2SLS
Logged annual delay	−0.0108**	−0.0245**	−0.0076	−0.0258**	−0.0101	−0.0178*
(Robust standard error)	(0.0046)	(0.0098)	(0.0079)	(0.0100)	(0.0089)	(0.0107)
Sample size	256	256	256	256	256	256
R^2	0.73	0.72	0.73	0.72	0.63	0.63

*$p < 0.1$; **$p < 0.05$; ***$p < 0.01$

Note: Robust standard errors account for clustering at the urban-area level of an unbalanced panel. All regressions include a full set of urban-area and year dummies, as well as a control for urban-area population size.

increases travel time and that congestion may affect their productivity and job satisfaction. For example, in a study of a travel agency, Bloom and others (2015) finds that remote workers were 22 percent more productive than their office-bound colleagues, who commuted to work, because they took fewer breaks and sick days, and that they were more satisfied with their jobs and less likely to leave the company. And a study of commuting and well-being in England found that a daily increase in commuting time of twenty minutes had the same negative effect on employee satisfaction as a 19 percent pay cut.[12] In the next section, we situate our estimates in a broader quantitative perspective.

For sensitivity analysis, we expand our controls in both stages to include interaction terms between urban areas and decades (1980–1989, 1990–1999, 2000–2009, and 2010–2012) to control for any longer-term structural shifts that might have occurred in specific urban areas, such as changes in population demographics. Not surprisingly, we find that the addition of those interaction terms reduces the precision of our estimates of the congestion effects because they add some thirty parameters to the specification, although they still have some statistical significance; however, the magnitudes of estimated congestion effects also tend to increase. We also conduct two other time-related sensitivity tests and find that the estimated congestion effects are robust.[13] Finally, we test the sensitivity of our job and wage growth models, which are based on county-level data that were transformed to urban-area data, with models based on MSA-level data that were transformed to urban-area data. We find only slightly smaller changes in the magnitude and statistical reliability of our estimated congestion effects on job and wage growth.

Congestion's Effect on Commodity-Freight Flows

As noted, we construct a measure of the three-year urban-area growth rate of freight traffic transported by truck across California counties. Because commodity traffic could be affected by congestion at the urban area of both its origin and destination, we instrument origin and destination congestion with each urban area's cumulative self-help highway revenue.

As shown in table 5-3, instrumenting congestion again increases the magnitude and statistical reliability of the congestion effect, as the 2SLS estimate of the effect of congestion at the origin on commodity-flow growth rates is statistically significant and is more than three times greater than the OLS estimate of the effect. We also find that the effect of congestion at the urban area of origin is roughly three times greater than the effect of congestion at the destination, which is not statistically significant, possibly because shippers may be able to avoid the logistics costs of certain congested destinations by shipping to less congested destinations instead of shipping less freight.

To transform the congestion elasticities for three-year growth rates into annualized elasticities, we simply divide the estimated originating urban area's congestion coefficient by 3 to obtain -0.106,

Table 5-3

Effects of Congestion on Logged Three-Year Interurban-Area Commodity-Flow Growth Rates

	OLS	2SLS
Logged annual delay at origin urban area	−0.0991[*]	−0.3184[**]
(Robust standard error)	(0.0389)	(0.1092)
Logged annual delay at destination urban area	−0.0053	−0.1179
(Robust standard error)	(0.0332)	(0.0732)
Sample size	100	100

[*] $p < 0.05$; [**] $p < 0.01$

Note: Robust standard errors were calculated using the Huber-White sandwich estimators. All regressions control for population size of the origin and destination urban areas. The R^2 for the OLS estimation was 0.09, which in all likelihood is lower than the R^2 for the preceding effects of congestion on growth rates because of the smaller sample size. The R^2 for the 2SLS estimation, which is arguably not informative, was not reported in STATA.

which is the largest congestion effect we find for an economic performance measure. This is perhaps because transportation, in terms of both time and out-of-pocket costs, is such an important component of trade costs (Anderson and van Wincoop 2004) and because increases in transportation costs that are reflected in higher prices may cause receivers to obtain freight from alternative origins.

For a sensitivity analysis of the model for commodity-flow growth, we include the distance between origin and destination urban areas and characteristics of the origin and destination urban areas in 2007, such as the number of four-year colleges, percentages of the populations that were African American, and percentages of the populations that were of working age (twenty to sixty-four). Our results are largely robust to the inclusion of those controls.

Bounding the Effect of Highway Congestion on the Performance Variables

We find that the magnitude of OLS estimates of the effect of highway congestion on the economic-performance measures is consistently smaller than the magnitude of the 2SLS estimates of that effect. Does the relative magnitude of the OLS and 2SLS estimates suggest that our instrument is controlling for the relevant unobserved variables that could cause biased and inconsistent estimates? Consider the OLS estimate of the effect of highway congestion on GDP growth. Congestion is procyclical because it generally increases with more economic activity. Thus unobserved variables that increase GDP growth are also likely to increase highway congestion, and this positive correlation would create a bias that reduces the negative effect of congestion on GDP growth. We argue that our instrumental variable purges much of the bias in the OLS coefficient and that this results empirically in a larger negative coefficient, as shown in table 5-2.

Do the 2SLS estimates therefore represent a lower bound on the effect of congestion on the performance variables? To address that question, we have to consider that there may be omitted variables that have a negative effect on GDP and are positively related to highway congestion, which would result in a negative correlation and an upward bias in the OLS estimates. Alternatively, an upward bias may result from omitted variables that have a positive effect on GDP and that are negatively related to highway congestion. It is therefore important to consider and control for those types of omitted variables, which would make it more likely that our instrumental-variable estimates represent a lower bound on the effect of congestion on the performance variables.

The most likely examples of omitted variables that have a positive effect on GDP and are negatively related to highway congestion are technological innovations, such as GPS navigation software that enables motorists and truckers to avoid incident delays caused by traffic accidents and other long congestion delays by recommending an alternative and faster route to their destination. Beginning in the mid-1990s, GPS navigation software was gradually introduced on certain vehicle makes, and its adoption has grown over time. Thus we reestimated our first- and second-stage models with time trends to control for the effect of navigational advances on highway travel delays. But we found that the effect of congestion on the performance variables was unaffected.

The most likely examples of omitted variables that have a negative effect on GDP and that are positively related to congestion are natural disasters such as the October 1989 Loma Prieta earthquake, which caused a major section of the Oakland Bay Bridge to collapse, disrupting economic activity throughout the Bay Area and increasing congestion delays.[14] Such natural events can be captured as random time-trend effects (as distinct from random effects and time trends). As a robustness check, we reestimated our models for the growth rate of GDP, jobs, and wages, using a specification that controls for those effects.

As indicated in the previous chapter, our current model can be summarized as

$$\ln G_{it} = \gamma \times \ln C_{it} + X_{it}\beta + \phi_t + c_i + \varepsilon_{it}, \qquad (5\text{-}1)$$

where G_{it} is the growth rate of an economic performance measure in urban area i in year t, γ is the causal effect of congestion level C on the growth rate, $X\beta$ is an array of controls and coefficients, ϕ_t is the year dummy, c_i is the urban-area dummy, and ε is the random error term. This model assumes that unobserved differences across urban areas are controlled for by urban-area fixed effects. If we expect that highway congestion and a performance growth-rate variable in an urban area are affected by unobserved factors over time, then the year dummies would capture only the time trend that is common across all urban areas.

To control for individual urban-area time trends (that is, random time-trend effects), we can specify

$$\ln G_{it} = \gamma \times \ln C_{it} + X_{it}\beta + \phi \times Trend + \theta_i \times Trend\, c_i + \varepsilon_{it}, \qquad (5\text{-}2)$$

where $\phi \times Trend$ captures the common time trend across the urban areas and $\theta_i \times Trend$, with θ_i random, allows each urban area to have its own time trend. To estimate the model, we use first-order differencing and demeaning to eliminate the urban-area time trends and dummies so that the remaining parameters can be consistently estimated by 2SLS, using the self-help highway taxes as our instrumental variable.[15]

We find that the estimated coefficients of the effects of congestion in those models are broadly consistent with, albeit somewhat larger than, the baseline coefficients presented in table 5-2.[16] But their precision is less than that of the baseline estimates because first-order differencing and demeaning reduced the variation in the data, so we will use the baseline coefficients for further analysis.

6

Simulation of the Effects of Autonomous Vehicles on Congestion

Autonomous vehicles represent a positive exogenous technological shock that has the potential to significantly reduce congestion and delays by improving traffic flows and reducing accidents. Reductions in delays could have direct positive effects on the growth rates of economic-performance measures.

Fagnant and Kockelman (2015) provides figures that we use to make a base-case assumption of the effect of autonomous vehicles on congestion. The authors report that at a 50 percent penetration (meaning that 50 percent of the vehicles on the road are autonomous), autonomous vehicles would cause a 35 percent reduction in freeway delays, accounting for the offsetting effect of induced travel, and would cause a 10 percent reduction in arterial delays. However, autonomous-vehicle penetration would be much greater in the longer run, and the authors report that at 90 percent penetration, autonomous vehicles would cause a 60 percent reduction in freeway delays, again accounting for the offsetting effect of induced travel, and a 15 percent reduction in arterial delays. We thus assume for our base-case simulation for California that widespread use of autonomous vehicles would lead to a 50 percent reduction in delays. We then perform a sensitivity analysis where we assume that the reduction in delays for the nation is 20 percent lower than the reduction in delays that we assume for California.[1]

Simulation Methodology

We estimate the significant potential improvements in the U.S. economy's performance that are attributable to autonomous vehicles' impact on congestion by developing counterfactual scenarios. We assume in those scenarios that autonomous vehicles would not induce more traffic that increases congestion, but we discuss that issue in more detail in a later chapter, when we consider congestion pricing in the context of widespread adoption of autonomous vehicles. For now, we suggest that it is possible that concerns about induced demand may be overstated if shared self-driving cars reduce the number of cars on the road as people opt to eliminate the costs of car ownership (Claudel and Ratti 2015), empty vehicles can be moved flexibly on routes and times of day to reduce their effect on delays, and travelers' heterogeneous preferences spread out the flow of traffic more than expected. For example, some commuters may adjust their schedules and leave earlier for work because they can have breakfast in their self-driving car, or they may leave later because they can accomplish certain work-related tasks while they are in their car.[2]

Ignoring, for simplicity, the urban-area fixed effects and subscript, as well as the time trend and subscript, we model congestion's effect on the growth rate of an economic-performance measure as

$$\ln(G) = \gamma \times \ln(C) + X\beta + \varepsilon, \tag{6-1}$$

where γ is the causal effect of congestion level C on growth rate G, $X\beta$ is an array of controls and coefficients, and ε is the random error term. In each counterfactual, we reduce congestion by $(100 \times \alpha)$ percent owing to the adoption of autonomous vehicles, and we assume that all else remains constant. Our postintervention growth rate is

$$\ln(G_{post}) = \gamma \times \ln(C \times (1 - \alpha)) + X\beta + \varepsilon. \qquad (6\text{-}2)$$

Subtracting equation 6-1 from equation 6-2 to obtain the difference in growth rates gives

$$\ln(G_{post}) - \ln(G) = [\gamma \times \ln(C \times (1 - \alpha)) + X\beta + \varepsilon] - [\gamma \times \ln(C) + X\beta + \varepsilon]$$

$$\ln(G_{post}) - \ln(G) = \gamma \times [\ln(C \times (1 - \alpha)) - \ln(C)]$$

$$\ln(G_{post}) - \ln(G) = \gamma \times \ln(1 - \alpha).$$

We can therefore express the postintervention growth rate as

$$G_{post} = G \times e^{\gamma \ln(1 - \alpha)}. \qquad (6\text{-}3)$$

Note that the postintervention growth rate for a given performance measure is not a function of the congestion level. Instead, it can be predicted from the actual growth rate of the performance measure (G), our estimate of the effect of congestion γ, and our base-case assumption, based on Fagnant and Kockelman (2015), that the adoption of autonomous vehicles would cause congestion delays to be reduced 50 percent ($\alpha = 0.50$).

We first determine the effects of autonomous vehicles on employment, real GDP, and labor-earnings growth for 2010. Actual 2010 and 2011 measures of economic performance are from the Bureau of Economic Analysis.[3] Counterfactual 2011 levels of economic performance are estimated by computing the appropriate G_{post} using equation 6-3 and then multiplying G_{post} by the actual 2010 level to derive a counterfactual 2011 level of economic performance. Actual 2011 levels are then subtracted from counterfactual 2011 levels to estimate the number of, say, jobs added in 2010 resulting from the assumed reduction in congestion.

Because we have commodity-flow data only for the years 2007 and 2010, we determine the effects of autonomous vehicles on California urban-area commodity flows for the year 2007.[4] We simulate the effect of congestion at the urban area of origin only because the estimated coefficient for congestion at the destination urban area was not statistically significant. Finally, because we do not account for the effect of congestion on freight flows to urban areas outside California, we understate the benefits to California from additional commodity flows.

To be sure, our simulations should be qualified because we are considering a very large reduction in congestion that has not occurred in our sample and because a disruptive technology that generates a large stimulus may activate various macroeconomic responses, including actions by the Federal Reserve; thus the positive effects might be transformed in various ways. For example, the workforce might enjoy more wage growth and less job growth if, in fact, the United States were close to full employment. Accordingly, a dynamic macroeconomic simulation is more likely to fully capture the effects of autonomous vehicles on the U.S. economy than a simulation based on a reduced-form model of the determinants of congestion. Nevertheless, we believe that the findings presented here are at least suggestive of the magnitude of those effects.

Simulation Results

Table 6-1 shows the potentially large benefits to California from motorists' adoption of autonomous vehicles, as a 50 percent reduction in congestion in 2010 would have enabled California to create nearly 350,000 additional jobs, increase its real GDP by $35 billion, and raise workers' earnings nearly $15 billion. In 2007 an additional $57 billion in commodities would have been shipped across its urban areas. Autonomous vehicles would raise few distributional concerns among travelers because all motorists could benefit from the new technology.

However, because the technology is disruptive, the adoption of autonomous vehicles could alter the structure of the economy by displacing some jobs and services, such as taxi drivers, public-transit workers, and (to a large extent) automobile-insurance com-

Table 6-1.

Counterfactual Estimates for California (units as indicated)

	Driverless cars reduce congestion by 50 percent
Jobs	
Increase in annual growth rate owing to reduced congestion (percent)	1.7
Actual employment level in 2010 (number of jobs)	19,806,213
Actual employment level in 2011 (number of jobs)	20,175,357
Counterfactual employment level in 2011 (number of jobs)	20,520,903
Jobs added in 2011 owing to reduced congestion	345,546
Real GDP	
Increase in annual growth rate owing to reduced congestion (percent)	1.8
Actual GDP level in 2010 (millions of dollars)	1,936,801
Actual GDP level in 2011 (millions of dollars)	1,960,153
Counterfactual GDP level in 2011 (millions of dollars)	1,995,522
Real GDP added in 2011 owing to reduced congestion (millions of dollars)	35,369
Real labor earnings	
Increase in annual growth rate owing to reduced congestion (percent)	1.2
Actual total wages in 2010 (thousands of dollars)	1,131,005,175
Actual total wages in 2011 (thousands of dollars)	1,165,682,489
Counterfactual total wages in 2011 (thousands of dollars)	1,180,153,793
Wages added in 2011 owing to reduced congestion (millions of dollars)	14,471
Intra-California commodity flows	
Increase in annual growth rate owing to reduced congestion (percent)	7.6
Actual value of commodity freight flows in 2007 (millions of dollars)	866,837
Actual value of commodity freight flows in 2008 (millions of dollars)	748,346
Counterfactual value of commodity freight flows in 2008 (millions of dollars)	805,400
Freight value added in 2008 owing to reduced congestion (millions of dollars)	57,054

panies and their employees, which contribute less social value in a much safer automated-driving environment. We discuss the effect of autonomous vehicles on displaced workers as well as its potential to create new jobs in the next chapter. Here, we simply provide perspective on the difficulty of predicting the employment effects of technological advance by recalling that ATMs were expected to put most bank tellers out of work. But in fact, ATMs contributed to the opening of more bank branches during the 1990s, and teller employment has actually increased over the past forty years (Bessen 2015). In any case, we acknowledge that any job loss that does occur would reduce the benefits from autonomous vehicles.

If the well-known saying, "As California goes, so goes the country," is correct, then the adoption of autonomous vehicles is likely to be a significant macroeconomic stimulus for the United States. We apply the same methodology and assumptions as before to predict the effects of a nationwide adoption of autonomous vehicles on U.S. employment, real GDP, and labor-earnings growth rates.[5] However, in comparison with other states, California has some of the worst congestion, the fewest transit options, and generally the greatest reliance on automobiles; thus congestion could plausibly have bigger impacts on growth in California than elsewhere. We cannot derive the appropriate scaling of benefits to account for heterogeneity across the nation, so as a starting point for discussion we also provide countrywide estimates, where we assume that the effect of autonomous vehicles on congestion is 20 percent lower for the United States as a whole than for California.

Extrapolating our California congestion effects to the United States, we find that the benefits to the nation are roughly nine times greater than the benefits to California. As shown in the first column of table 6-2, autonomous vehicles could generate 3 million additional jobs; this would raise the nation's annual growth rate by 1.8 percentage points from a 2010 baseline GDP of about $14.6 trillion and raise annual labor earnings by more than $100 billion.[6] The absence of data on interstate commodity-freight flows prevents us from esti-

Table 6-2

Counterfactual Estimates for the United States (millions of dollars)

	Assuming California congestion effects	Assuming 80 percent of California congestion effects
Jobs added in 2011 owing to reduced congestion	3,019,284	2,411,318
Real GDP added in 2011 owing to reduced congestion	267,848	213,894
Labor earnings added in 2011 owing to reduced congestion	112,364	89,780

mating the nationwide trade flow increases caused by a significant reduction in congestion, but they are certain to be large.[7]

If we assume that highway congestion reductions from autonomous vehicles in the United States would have 80 percent of the economic boost that they would have in California, the benefits of autonomous vehicles would still be strikingly large, as indicated in the second column of table 6-2, which shows that the increase in the nation's annual growth rate would amount to 1.4 percentage points.[8] If we make a stronger assumption about the effects of autonomous vehicles on reducing congestion, such as that they are 50 percent lower for the United States as a whole than for California, then autonomous vehicles would still generate significant improvements in the nation's annual rate of growth, approaching 1 percentage point. At this point, we should recognize that this estimate is clearly an underestimate of the effect of autonomous vehicles on economic growth because we have not accounted for the effect of autonomous vehicles on improving the reliability of travel, which would reduce another cost of distance, and we have omitted from the estimation other important potential benefits of autonomous vehicles that are discussed in the next chapter.

It may seem implausible that such improvements in highway travel—significant as they are—could also have such large macroeconomic effects. However, the value of transportation networks, like that of other networks, increases according to Metcalf's Law in proportion to the square of the number of nodes in the network.[9] By increasing accessibility to more parts (nodes) of the network, a given reduction in travel costs (measured in money and time) would generate gains by manyfold; for example, a halving of travel costs raises the value of the transportation network sixteenfold.

Historically, the importance of improvements in mobility to the development of the U.S. economy has long been recognized. For example, Krugman (2009) explains how this country's railroads, by reducing transportation costs and the costs of distance, facilitated large-scale production (economies of scale) and transformed the U.S. economy into a differentiated farm belt and manufacturing belt. A century later, the construction of the interstate highway system generated an annualized welfare gain of 1.4 percent of GDP (Allen and Arkolakis 2014).

To be sure, today's transportation system has evolved considerably from the systems that were in place when railroad service became available in the 1800s and when the interstate system was built during the 1950s (Winston 2010). Congestion on the nation's roads has significantly increased, to the point where its effect on a modest part of the U.S. transportation system can have a large effect on GNP. For example, Amiti and others (2015) calculates that congestion at the nation's West Coast ports, which occurred from July 2014 through February 2015, while dockworkers and marine terminal employers were negotiating a contract, caused perishable agricultural commodities to go bad, resulting in a 0.2 percentage point reduction in GDP growth during the first quarter of 2015.

Given that a considerable amount of the nation's inputs (labor and capital) and outputs are transported on local, state, and federal roads, it is plausible that a large decline in congestion that is caused by a major technological advance in the modes that use the road system could affect the nation's economic growth by a similar order of magnitude as the development of the federal interstate highway system. While we have argued that the effects of autonomous vehicles on congestion represent their largest potential economic benefit, autonomous vehicles have the potential to produce several other large economic and social benefits as well.

7

Other Important Effects of Autonomous Vehicles

The technological benefit of autonomous vehicles is that they have the potential to reduce some of the adverse effects of cars and trucks—we have shown the potentially huge benefits from their effects on reducing congestion—and to increase those modes' positive effects. In this chapter, we discuss the effect of autonomous vehicles on improving traffic safety, health, accessibility, land use, employment, the efficiency of the U.S. transportation system, and public finance. When we summarize all the potential benefits of autonomous vehicles in the conclusion, the importance of our central thesis becomes crystal clear: policymakers must take effective actions to take full advantage of this extraordinary technological advance.

Traffic Safety

According to NHTSA, the annual social costs from motor-vehicle crashes are approaching $1 trillion, accounting for economic losses, loss of life, and pain and suffering (NHTSA 2015). In recent years, some 40,000 people have been killed in car and truck crashes, roughly 4 million injured, and about 25 million vehicles damaged.

By eliminating human error and risky driving behavior, the primary causes of accidents, autonomous vehicles can generate enormous social benefits, including the gradual elimination of most, and eventually all, of the cost of motor-vehicle personal and property insurance as states drop mandatory coverage regulations.[1]

The technological issues surrounding the development of safe and reliable autonomous vehicles and the available evidence on how those vehicles would improve the safety of nonautonomous vehicles are discussed later. As a preview, the evidence indicates that trading off the fallibility of artificial intelligence for the fallibility of human judgment and decisionmaking would result in a dramatic improvement in highway safety that would be broadly shared among all members of society. There is some ambiguity, however, about the optimal time to allow the public to adopt autonomous vehicles— that is, whether they should be made available to the public when they are determined to be completely safe for travelers to use or whether they should be made available earlier, even if some uncertainty about their safety remains, because allowing the public to travel in those vehicles could still save lives. Kalra and Groves (2017) develops a framework to show that the timing of the public's adoption of autonomous vehicles cannot avoid this tradeoff.

Health

Given the detrimental health effects of commuting, it is not surprising that surveys indicate that it is the leading activity over the course of the day for which individuals' dominant attitude is negative (Kahneman and Krueger 2006). Several studies have explored how automobile commuting, especially in congested conditions, can damage adults' and infants' physical and emotional health and well-being, with such suggestive titles as: "5 Ways Commuting Ruins Your Life" (Fottrell 2015), "Caution, Drivers! Children Present" (Knittel, Miller, and Sanders 2016), and *Health in a Hurry* (Royal Society for Public Health 2017).

Congestion can also reduce health by increasing pollution. Simeonova and others (2018) finds that Stockholm's congestion tax reduced not only congestion but also ambient air pollution, which was associated with a significant decrease in the rate of acute asthma attacks among young children. Finally, congestion has been associated with an increase in crime. Beland and Brent (2017) finds that traffic above the 95th percentile increased the incidence of domestic violence, a crime that has been shown to be affected by emotional stress, which could be caused by driving in highly congested conditions.

Autonomous vehicles could therefore produce additional benefits in the form of improved emotional health of motorists, less domestic violence, and greater productivity because commuters would not be driving and would be traveling in less congested conditions. Travelers in autonomous vehicles would benefit from a reduction in travel time and also in the disutility of travel time, because highway travel would become a more pleasant experience, although the reduction in the disutility of travel time would imply that the travel-time savings would become less valuable (van den Berg and Verhoef 2016).

Public health would also improve, because the reduction in congestion and stop-and-go driving would reduce tailpipe emissions. Combining autonomous with electric vehicles would improve air quality even further. And, if autonomous vehicles could be made almost perfectly safe, it may be socially desirable to reduce their crashworthiness by reducing their weight, which would improve energy efficiency.

Autonomous-vehicle use would also improve public health and safety in off-peak periods, especially late at night: police would not be stopping vehicles for speeding or driving erratically, thereby reducing the likelihood of a potentially violent confrontation and allowing police to focus on other public safety concerns.[2] Finally, autonomous cars and trucks could be much more difficult—or could be designed to be more difficult—for terrorists to use to carry out attacks on crowds of people by, for example, programming them so that they are prevented from driving off conventional thoroughfares and going into such areas.

Accessibility

By improving travel time and reliability, autonomous vehicles would improve accessibility by enabling travelers and freight to reach their destinations faster. In addition, by providing greater access to local and intercity destinations, autonomous vehicles could help raise earnings for people who face economic disadvantages, enable people who cannot drive to take more trips, and significantly reduce the risks of accidents caused by people who are allowed to drive but who potentially pose special risks to others on the road.

Smart and Klein (2015) finds that carless households could raise their incomes if they had access to a car to improve their employment opportunities, but they also find that the cost of a new or used car is generally higher than the possible income gain. Public transit does not provide much of an alternative: Tomer (2012) documents that it enables commuters to reach less than one-third of metrowide jobs within ninety minutes.[3] However, autonomous vehicles, which could be owned or hired at a lower cost than nonautonomous vehicles because their insurance costs would be much lower, among other considerations, would be readily available to any commuter and could therefore expand employment opportunities and increase earnings of carless households.

Autonomous vehicles could enable people who are prohibited from driving, because of age or infirmity, to travel alone in a car without endangering themselves and others. During the transition from nonautonomous to autonomous-vehicle use, autonomous vehicles could also enable people who are prohibited from driving a nonautonomous vehicle because their license has been revoked or suspended to travel in an autonomous vehicle without posing a possible threat to traffic safety.

Finally, elderly people and people who drive long distances, such as truck drivers, may be legally allowed to drive but may be unwilling to confront the dangers they pose to themselves and others on the road because they ignore the decline in their cognitive functioning or because they are committed to reaching their destinations on time, even if they are extremely tired. As the population continues to age, owing to the reduction in mortality at older ages, the threat to highway safety caused by cognitive decline will be exacerbated. For example, people ninety and older now make up 4.7 percent of the elderly population (sixty-five and older), and their share is likely to reach 10 percent by 2050.[4] Given the potential availability of autonomous vehicles, elderly people will not have to wrestle with the decision whether to give up driving, and people who make long-distance trips by car or truck will not have to struggle with staying awake to avoid getting into an accident.

Land Use

The automobile had a significant impact on society by enabling people to live farther from their place of work in larger, less expensive houses on larger lots. But in urban areas that experienced congestion, the value of properties closer to workplaces significantly increased, and cities implemented land-use policies, such as zoning, to limit metropolitan growth and congestion. At the same time, to accommodate the need for parking space in residential and business areas, cities implemented additional land-use policies, such as minimum-parking requirements, to ensure that sufficient parking was available. Currently, the United States has more parking spaces than cars, and many of those spaces are free or highly subsidized.[5] In New York City, for example, parking covers an area equivalent to two Central Parks (Sidders and Shankleman 2018).

Land-use policies have raised housing prices by reducing the quantity of housing available for purchase or rent in two ways: by reducing the land that is available for new housing and is instead used for parking, and by limiting the amount and type of housing that can be constructed on the available land. Raising the price of housing discourages people from relocating to new areas, especially productive areas of the country, such as the San Francisco Bay and New York metropolitan areas, that pay higher wages. Economic growth goes hand in hand with an enormous reallocation of the population. Albouy and Stuart (2016), Herkenhoff, Ohanian, and Prescott (2018), and Hsieh and Moretti (2018) report empirical evidence that land-use policies that have discouraged households from relocating to other parts of the country have significantly reduced GDP.

Autonomous-vehicle use could increase GDP by improving land use in two ways: space that is currently used for parking could be used instead for construction of additional housing, and reduced congestion would help to justify elimination of zoning policies that are allegedly intended to help reduce congestion but that, in practice, restrict construction of new housing units.

Nourinejad, Bahrami, and Roorda (2018) notes that autonomous vehicles could significantly reduce the parking footprint for suburban malls and make land available for housing, because drivers leave their vehicles at the parking entrance or at designated drop-off zones, and the vehicle could be directed to a spot chosen by the car-park operator. The authors estimate that the average parking space per vehicle in car parks would decrease by two square meters per vehicle because the driving lanes would become narrower, elevators and staircases would become obsolete, and the required room for opening a vehicle's doors would become unnecessary. The efficient use of car-park space would be further enhanced by stacking the vehicles in several rows, one behind the other, with an optimal layout to ensure smooth retrieval of a vehicle when a user summons it.

Autonomous vehicles would also free up considerable space in downtown areas, space that is currently used for parking lots and on-street parking, for additional housing or for productive economic activity that potentially increases agglomeration economies. Again, autonomous vehicles could let passengers off at their destinations and be parked in optimally configured garages on the outskirts of town, especially if the vehicles were shared instead of owned.[6] Traffic would therefore not be impeded by drivers cruising for parking places.[7]

By significantly reducing congestion, autonomous vehicles would weaken the justification for land-use policies that imposed large costs in attempting to do so. A further benefit from a land-use perspective is that the reduced cost of commuting longer distances to work would encourage more people to live in less expensive, more spacious housing in the exurbs. Employers in certain areas with high housing prices have faced difficulties filling certain jobs or have been able to do so only if their employees are willing to make "extreme" commutes, at least ninety minutes each way (extreme commuters account for 3 percent of the nation's commuters). Autonomous vehicles could offer a faster, more relaxing commute for additional long-distance, but not necessarily extreme, commuters and could help clear the labor market in expensive metropolitan areas.

By encouraging people to move to the exurbs, it could be argued, autonomous vehicles would contribute to the costs of sprawl, including higher costs for city services, loss of open space, more carbon emissions, and so on. However, as discussed later, efficient public policies could reduce those costs.

Finally, the use of shared autonomous vehicles could also significantly reduce costly parking for renters. Gabbe and Pierce (2017) estimates that the cost of bundled garage parking for renters is approximately $1,700 per year; the cost of building garage spaces adds about 17 percent to a unit's rent; and more than 700,000 households do not have a car but pay higher rent because they have a garage parking space. Homeowners who share autonomous vehicles could use housing space that was formerly used for a garage for another worthwhile purpose or could reduce the size and cost of their house.

Labor

Disruptive technologies disrupt. They even disrupt labor markets. Workers and new entrants to the labor force may need to adjust as new jobs are created and as other sectors expand. Anxiety about the impact of automation on the labor force and workers' employment has had a long history in the United States. The introduction of the automobile in the early 1900s provoked criticism that it would eliminate jobs, such as shoveling horse manure from public thoroughfares. By the 1950s, concerns about automation led *The Nation* to coin the term "automation depression." However, the recession of 1957–1958 did not last long, and it was followed by a strong recovery in which business was given credit for leading the expansion, but government policy to assist displaced workers was viewed, and has continued to be viewed, as ineffective (Wartzman 2017).

Acemoglu and Restrepo (2019) provides a general discussion of how automation affects the demand for labor. Automation reduces the demand for workers, as capital substitutes for labor. But it increases the demand for labor for nonautomated tasks by increasing productivity. In addition, automation creates new tasks in which labor has a comparative advantage. The authors report that about half of the employment growth over the 1980–2015 period took place in occupations in which job titles or tasks performed by workers changed. And since 2007, the e-commerce sector has created more jobs than brick-and-mortar retailers have lost.[8]

Automation may be a threat to jobs when labor-force participation is high, but it may be a solution to excess demand for labor when labor-force participation is low, which may characterize the U.S. workforce for the foreseeable future. According to the Bureau of Labor Statistics, after reaching its historical peak of 67.1 percent in 2000, the labor-force-participation rate for all workers (age sixteen and over) is projected to decline to 61.0 percent in 2026, primarily as a result of an aging population.[9] The trucking industry, for example, is already feeling the effects of a declining labor-force-participation rate; it is experiencing an excess demand for drivers as older drivers are retiring and fewer young people are entering the profession. Trucking productivity is also being affected by hours-of-service rules that limit driving time during a twenty-four-hour period.

Notwithstanding long-run structural considerations, 3.8 million workers, 3 percent of total U.S. employment, drive for a living, while 11.7 million workers drive as part of their work, including personal-care aids, police officers, and the like, according to occupational data from the Department of Commerce. Employment among the latter group of workers is unlikely to be affected much by autonomous vehicles because those workers still need to get places as part of their underlying jobs. However, the widespread adoption of autonomous vehicles is likely to force many drivers of trucks, buses, rail transit, taxis, and shared-transportation services such as Uber and Lyft to look for new jobs. At the same time, trucking productivity, in particular, will increase because the vehicle will constantly be moving.[10]

Although there will be fewer jobs in the driver's seat, some drivers will be needed to provide security for a vehicle's cargo and to handle certain logistical matters, while additional jobs will develop at transportation centers that monitor the autonomous-road network and respond to public inquiries. Jobs will also develop to maintain, repair, and clean autonomous vehicles that are hired and owned, to handle customer service, and to keep maps for optimal routings updated.

For example, in 2019, Waymo announced that it was seeking to fill jobs for its new self-driving taxi service in Phoenix in the following, effectively new, job categories:

- technicians for vehicle inspections and repairs

- dispatchers to handle the logistics of ensuring that enough vehicles are on the road

- fleet response teams to handle difficult situations should they arise on the road

- customer service representatives to field calls from passengers at any time

Similar jobs will be created when companies start to provide autonomous delivery services. Viscelli (2018) concludes that the current jobs most at risk of displacement are long-distance-driving jobs with few specialized tasks, representing fewer than 300,000 drivers. Yankelevich and others (2018) reaches a similar conclusion.[11]

The shift from owning to sharing vehicles may actually turn out to increase total production and employment in the automobile industry. On the one hand, vehicle use will be much greater, and far fewer vehicles will be left idle. At the same time, it is likely that a plethora of specialized vehicles will be developed over time in response to travelers' preferences. For example, certain vehicles designed for work trips might have a conference table with adequate seating capacity for meetings; vehicles that specialize in local shopping trips might have flexible capacity to carry different kinds of cargo; specialty vehicles for long-distance pleasure trips could facilitate sleeping; and the like. Thus the reduction in production of "standard" vehicles may be offset by new production of specialized vehicles that are shared.

Different types of autonomous vehicles could facilitate new services and increase employment. For example, autonomous vehicles could be used to provide restaurant and even hotel service for people while traveling, free transportation to increase turnout at certain events or patronage at certain stores, and trucking services that use drones, if necessary, to provide the last-mile delivery.

The development of specialty vehicles and new services suggests that autonomous vehicles could create positive spillover employment effects. For example, as people are able to consume individualized content during their drive and as new viewing technologies are developed to enable consumers to enjoy their drive time more, internet and media companies might experience growth in demand. Other industries that are likely to gain jobs include telecommunications, because firms in the industry will play a crucial role in facilitating data flow that is necessary to ensure the safety and efficiency of a system of autonomous vehicles, and electronics, computer science, and chemistry, because research advances by companies in those industries would affect and be affected by the evolution of autonomous vehicles (Giarratana 2018). Finally, when autonomous electric vehicles are adopted, additional electricity, charging stations, and semiconductors will be necessary, which will create more jobs by increasing the output of utilities, telecommunications operators, and chipmakers.

Kane and Tomer (2018) provides a rough estimate that the autonomous-vehicle industry—that is, digital mobility—could employ nearly 10 million workers. In addition, because the technology would improve accessibility to jobs, enhance job matching, and generate economic growth, widespread use of autonomous vehicles could lead to additional employment outside of digital mobility. Although it is always difficult to predict the effects that a new technology will have on employment, the many positive effects of autonomous vehicles on jobs are likely to offset the loss in employment among displaced drivers and possibly among certain automobile production workers.[12]

Other Modes of Transportation

The significant service and cost advantages of autonomous vehicles will pose formidable competitive challenges to other modes of freight and passenger transportation, thereby improving the efficiency of the U.S. transportation system. In addition, autonomous vehicles may facilitate the transition to electric vehicles.

Freight modes. Autonomous trucks, which are being developed and tested in the United States and elsewhere, will intensify truck competition with freight railroads for freight traffic.[13] In all likelihood, trucking operations will evolve to full autonomy. For example, trucking companies may initially adopt automated-vehicle platooning, with one driver leading many autonomous trucks on highways. Those vehicles would move large volumes of freight with much fewer workers, reducing labor costs and serving to address the growing shortage of qualified commercial truck drivers. Even when trucks operate autonomously on highways, there may be a driver meeting a truck at a highway exit to finish the journey on city streets. Eventually, autonomous trucks would complete the entire journey on highways and city streets.

In response, railroads are likely to adopt some form of autonomous technology to compete effectively with autonomous trucks and to continue to perform intermodal operations. Generally, the improvement in the cost and service quality of the surface-freight modes will reduce firms' inventory costs and will simplify transportation logistics because shippers' supply chains will be continually active.

Public transit. Public transit suffers from enormous operating inefficiencies, caused in part by regulations, huge deficits, and declining ridership, which has led some studies (Winston and Shirley 1998; Winston and Maheshri 2007) to question transit's social desirability—that is, whether transit's benefits to users and its contribution to reducing congestion are outweighed by its ever-growing annual operating and capital subsidies, which currently exceed $25 billion.[14]

The recent entry of transportation network companies, such as Uber and Lyft, into the urban transportation market has hastened the decline in public-transit ridership. Graehler, Mucci, and Erhardt (2019) finds that each year after transportation network companies enter a market, heavy-rail ridership can be expected to decrease 1.3 percent and bus ridership to decrease 1.7 percent. The authors find that the transportation network companies' effect builds with each passing year.

As noted, it is quite likely that a large share of the population would no longer own but would instead choose to rent or share an autonomous car when needed, which would be less costly than incurring the capital cost of vehicle ownership. Thus autonomous shared vehicles would eventually become the dominant mode of urban transportation. Competition from those vehicles would be even more intense than the competition provided by nonautonomous transportation network companies. It would reduce public-transit's ridership levels to the point where its social desirability was no longer in doubt and would justify eliminating its subsidies, thereby benefiting taxpayers, and ending its operations, because virtually every traveler would have access to a low-cost and personalized alternative. Some public transit systems would probably experiment with autonomous transit vehicles in an attempt to reduce labor costs, but even that adjustment is unlikely to attract sufficient patronage to enable most transit systems to be economically viable in a world of autonomous vehicles.[15]

Taxis. Transportation network companies have also taken a large share of conventional taxis' patronage and have caused many drivers to suffer severe financial distress. For example, the value of a taxi medallion in New York City has fallen from a high of more than $1 million in 2013 to less than $200,000 in 2018. Clearly, taxis will cease operations when, if not before, autonomous vehicles are widely adopted.

Electric vehicles. It is likely that autonomous vehicles will eventually be combined with electric vehicles to create autonomous electric vehicles. Shared autonomous vehicles may facilitate the transition to electric vehicles by reducing the time costs to consumers of recharging, because a fully-charged autonomous electric vehicle would generally be provided to consumers by a shared vehicle company. In addition, households would not have to invest in costly charging stations at home.

Modes in development. Finally, the lessons that policymakers and the public learn from society's transition to and adoption of autonomous vehicles are likely to be useful as society considers the use of other autonomous transportation modes that are currently being developed by the private sector, including robot delivery services, drones, and even flying cars.[16] All of those modes have the potential to become viable components of the U.S. transportation system: they are receiving significant funding from private investors, are well along in their technical development, and are being tested in advance of plausible commercial operations. They offer significant potential benefits to the public by further reducing the cost of distance, but they also face significant technological and policy challenges, many of which are similar to those that autonomous vehicles must overcome to succeed.

Public Finance of Roads

The nation's dependence on funding from a federal gasoline tax that has been fixed since 1993, despite improvements in the fuel economy of the nation's vehicle fleet, has caused the federal Highway Trust Fund to run a deficit that is likely to grow for the foreseeable future. Policymakers have called the combination of travel conditions on deteriorating highways and insufficient funds to ameliorate them an infrastructure crisis.

Autonomous vehicles can improve travel conditions, but their improved fuel economy from traveling in a smoother traffic flow with much less stop-and-go driving will reduce gasoline tax revenues to finance government highway expenditures (Adler, Peer, and Sinozic 2018; Ratner 2018). Funding problems will become more severe when the public starts to adopt autonomous electric vehicles. In fact, the tiny share of electric-vehicle owners in Illinois must now pay $248 a year to make up for lost gas-tax revenue. However, the silver lining of the funding shortfalls is that they will strengthen the case for a comprehensive policy of efficient road pricing of autonomous vehicles and improve the political attractiveness of the policy.

Summary

Because the potential benefits from autonomous vehicles are so extensive, the public and policymakers may not appreciate all of them and may therefore underestimate the overall benefits of autonomous vehicles to society. At the same time, the public and policymakers may perceive the costs of autonomous vehicles to be greater than they are likely to be when those vehicles are widely adopted, because they do not consider effective responses that could ameliorate those costs. Although most of the potential benefits cannot be quantified at this point, there are a number of ways they could eventually be measured, which provides a qualitative sense of their importance.

By reducing congestion, autonomous vehicles could increase the annual growth rate of GDP by at least 1 percentage point. And by virtually eliminating 40,000 annual fatalities with an economic value of a statistical life of at least $10 million dollars,[17] autonomous vehicles could generate some $400 billion in safety benefits per year. Virtually eliminating nonfatal injuries and vehicle damage from collisions and reducing insurance costs would significantly add to those benefits.

Autonomous vehicles could improve the emotional health of travelers, reduce domestic violence and police confrontations, and make it much more difficult for terrorists to use a vehicle to attack a crowd of people. Autonomous vehicles could also improve health by reducing emissions. As autonomous vehicles are adopted and their effects on pollution are measured, researchers can quantify those gains in terms of the value of the reduction in deaths and illnesses that can be attributed to less pollution.

Autonomous vehicles could improve the quality of life and earnings for people who cannot drive or who have little access to transportation. Those benefits could be measured by the value of the new trips that those people take.

Autonomous vehicles could generate benefits that are measured by the value of urban land that is currently used for on-street parking and parking garages, making it available for more productive uses. Additional benefits would arise by eliminating inefficient land-use policies, which would help to reduce housing prices and spur an efficient reallocation of labor. Autonomous vehicles could allow less stressful and faster long-distance commutes, which could benefit workers who live far from their workplaces in lower cost housing.

Autonomous vehicles could increase the demand for labor for nonautomated tasks by increasing productivity and could create new tasks in which labor has a comparative advantage.

The overall efficiency of the U.S. transportation system would be enhanced as autonomous trucks and eventually autonomous railroads improved their operations, urban transportation was provided by only efficient suppliers, and subsidies for inefficient public transit services were reduced, if not eliminated.

Clearly, the total benefits to the United States that autonomous vehicles could potentially generate are staggering. At the same time, their negative effects on land use, employment, other modes, and public finance could be significantly reduced if transportation officials implement efficient highway policies.

Part 3

Constraints on the Success of Autonomous Vehicles

8

Technological Constraints

Policymakers and the public must be convinced that autonomous vehicles are safe; otherwise, their adoption will be severely limited or postponed indefinitely. The new technology has its critics. Kalra and Paddock (2016) argues that autonomous vehicles would have to travel hundreds of millions (possibly hundreds of billions) of miles before their reliability and safety could be fully determined. But the study assumes that autonomous-vehicle software and technology are static and ignores suppliers' steep learning curve, where, as exemplified by Waymo's simulation of challenging driving situations, driving mistakes can be quickly identified and corrected, and vehicles can learn from other vehicles' experience.[1]

Drawing on accident data based on the experience of nonautonomous vehicles, Fowles and Loeb (2018) concludes that autonomous vehicles have the potential to greatly improve safety by negating the primary factors that have contributed to fatalities involving nonautonomous vehicles; namely, driving under the influence of alcohol or drugs, while using a cellphone or other distracting device, with diminished reflexes, with limited experience, and in an aggressive or suicidal manner.

Drawing on the limited experience to date with autonomous vehicles in testing environments, the Insurance Institute for Highway Safety and the Virginia Tech Transportation Institute (Blanco and others 2016) find evidence that self-driving vehicles are involved in far fewer and less severe crashes than human-driven vehicles and that features that have already been installed in semiautonomous new cars, including lane drifting and vehicle blind-spot warnings, are significantly reducing accidents.[2] In nearly all cases in which autonomous vehicles were involved in accidents while conducting road tests, the accidents were caused by humans.

Finally, autonomous-vehicle suppliers are anticipating and taking steps to ensure safety in response to new problems, such as hacking and blinding.[3] For example, autonomous-vehicle suppliers are actively recruiting skilled security researchers and so-called white-hat hackers, who are paid to discover flaws in their vehicles' computer systems, to ensure against threats to security. Researchers are also experimenting with ways that LIDAR might be tricked to blind autonomous vehicles or to get them to react to apparent objects that are not in fact there, and then developing ways to defend the systems against such attacks.

Testing and actual experience with autonomous vehicles will continue to help automakers and technology companies identify unanticipated safety issues and to spur constructive solutions. The failure of policymakers to set up a national framework to test autonomous vehicles and to develop standards for those vehicles that all manufacturers must meet is delaying potential improvements in safety and the public's acceptance of the technology.

Autonomous vehicles have already been involved in collisions and fatal accidents, and there is no doubt that they will be involved in more accidents as the technology continues to be tested and perfected. The legal community has raised issues of product liability when those accidents occur, and they engage in debates with stakeholders over who will be held responsible in the event of a crash—the vehicle manufacturer, the tech company, the infrastructure operator, the vehicle owner, or the occupant—and consider whether responsibility could be apportioned, depending on the nature of the crash.

Kohler and Colbert-Taylor (2015), Smith (2017), Geistfeld (2018), and others provide overviews of those issues. Responsibility has yet to be established, and as in other cases of liability for new products, the law is likely to evolve as autonomous vehicles are adopted and the public gains greater experience with them. In the interim, it is important that legal concerns do not materially slow the implementation of autonomous-vehicle technology.

The moral issue of whether autonomous vehicles should be programmed to save passengers or pedestrians when they have a choice has also been raised (Bonnefon, Shariff, and Rahwan 2016). Obviously, this is a difficult issue to resolve before autonomous vehicles have been introduced, and it may not even be a valid concern except in very unusual circumstances, given significant advances in autonomous-vehicle technology.

Since the 1980s, the private sector has generally followed an orderly process to simultaneously develop and extensively test truly autonomous vehicles in actual driving situations before they are offered for hire or for sale to the public.[4] All indications are that the industry's massive effort to perfect the technology will bear fruit and that the technology will be safe and certainly an improvement over human operation when it is finally adopted on U.S. roads. At this point, there is no reason to believe that technological constraints will significantly limit or prevent autonomous vehicles from providing potentially enormous benefits to the nation.

9

Public-Policy Constraints

Policymakers will have considerable time to prepare the country—specifically, the highway infrastructure—for successful adoption of autonomous vehicles. However, early indications are that they are not fully committed to making progress to implement new policies and to reform existing ones, which could cause the adoption of autonomous vehicles to be delayed and their performance to be significantly compromised when they are adopted.

Policymakers must take four crucial steps to ensure safe and timely introduction:

- establish a framework for testing autonomous vehicles nationwide and set the standards that providers must meet to sell their vehicles to the public

- develop protocols for using autonomous vehicles while nonautonomous vehicles are still in use

- implement appropriate technology to facilitate autonomous vehicles' connectedness with one another and with highway infrastructure, the network, and possibly pedestrians

- reform current highway pricing, investment, and production policies that have significantly reduced the efficiency of nonautonomous vehicles for decades, so that the efficiency of autonomous-vehicle operations will not be similarly compromised

A Framework for Testing and Adoption

As described in chapter 2, in 2018 Congress drafted but failed to pass legislation that would have affirmed federal responsibility for the safety of autonomous vehicles through regulations of vehicle design and performance. In addition, it would have established a process whereby NHTSA could work with automakers and technology companies to establish safety and performance standards that a supplier would have to meet before it could sell its autonomous vehicles to the public.

The autonomous-vehicle industry has been frustrated by NHTSA's lack of aggressive support for federal regulatory legislation and by Congress's inability to pass the necessary legislation, and it is increasingly concerned that the legislation will be delayed further by a divided Congress. As an alternative, the industry is hoping that NHTSA may move policy forward by establishing a framework for regulating the safety of autonomous vehicles, which could facilitate testing throughout the country and possibly expedite eventual adoption.

In any case, congressional delays, along with the Trump administration's apparent disinterest in the matter, raise disturbing questions about policymakers' commitment to this potentially revolutionary technology that has the potential to produce enormous benefits for the country.[1] The five senators who have held up passage of legislation are allegedly concerned about the safety of the vehicles and how they will interact with their environment. At the same time, the lack of federal leadership and of a consistent testing standard has forced automakers and technology companies to navigate a patchwork of state regulations that range from strict, such as New York's requirement that state troopers trail self-driving test cars, to lax, such as those in Arizona and Florida that allow cars without drivers to be operated on public roads.

Congressional and NHTSA's inaction has not prevented testing from moving forward, however, and it has not been shown to be prudent caution, given the safety performance that autonomous vehicles have demonstrated in their tests on public roads. The primary effect of congressional and federal regulatory inaction has been to prevent the industry from learning about the safety performance of its vehicles as quickly as possible and in as many different driving environments as possible so that they can identify problems and take measures to correct problems.

Mixing Autonomous and Nonautonomous Vehicles in Traffic

During the transition to the full adoption of autonomous vehicles, which is likely to occur over a number of decades, there will be a period when nonautonomous vehicles are also being used on public roads. It will be important for policymakers to gradually allow for a mix of autonomous and nonautonomous vehicles in the flow of traffic and to segregate the vehicles when appropriate. Autonomous vehicles can coordinate with one another, and engineers are developing the technology to operate them with nonautonomous vehicles safely in mixed-traffic flow on local streets and arterials.

In the case of highways, autonomous vehicles may need to demonstrate their effectiveness and safety on dedicated autonomous-vehicle highways or highway lanes to reduce underuse of highway capacity.[2] China is building a new highway with dedicated lanes for autonomous vehicles. High-performance limited-access highways combine higher speeds with greater safety largely because the environment is simple and predictable: pedestrians are unlikely to jaywalk across an expressway, for example, and there are no parked cars or driveways along the side of the road. Popular fears about autonomous cars, and especially about autonomous trucks, are likely to largely vanish if only autonomous vehicles are on the road. Separated lanes offer added advantages by enabling the infrastructure to be designed specifically with autonomous vehicles in mind.

This is not to suggest a one-lane-at-a time building strategy for the entire U.S. highway system. A new autonomous-vehicle passenger-car lane, perhaps from San Jose to San Francisco, added to State Highway 101, could be a natural place to begin a nationwide demonstration of dedicated autonomous-vehicle lanes. Alternatively, large trucking companies could collectively commit to investing in autonomous trucks that could share a major dedicated route, perhaps from Chicago to Newark harbor. In this case, the trucking companies might operate the dedicated highway route as a cooperative.[3]

A precedent exists for dedicated lanes in the form of the high-occupancy toll or express toll lanes that are becoming increasingly popular with policymakers in various American states. Express toll lanes are open only to motorists who are willing to pay a toll, while high-occupancy toll lanes allow a motorist traveling in a carpool with at least one other person to use the lane for free. High-occupancy and express toll lanes are built in the median or alongside an expressway and are usually separated from the expressway's general-purpose lanes by physical barriers, although in a few cases they are separated only with pavement markings. Entrances to and exits from the express lanes are allowed only at designated points, where tolls are collected electronically. Tolls vary by time of day in an effort to maintain a minimum speed in the express lanes, and an increasing number of facilities use dynamic pricing, in which the tolls vary according to actual traffic volume and speed.[4]

Dedicated lanes for autonomous vehicles would be a more attractive option than express lanes for traditional vehicles because autonomous vehicles are likely to be superior to traditional vehicles in their comfort and performance. And the performance of autonomous vehicles would be enhanced if the autonomous vehicle lanes or highways were to feature distinct infrastructure to facilitate, for example, vehicle-to-vehicle communication. It would also be appropriate that the first autonomous vehicles operating in cities do so in separate lanes or even in separate autonomous-vehicle-only neighborhoods. After travelers have experience with and confidence in autonomous vehicles in dedicated environments, policymakers could turn to the more complex issue of allowing autonomous vehicles to operate on city streets simultaneously used, at least initially, by nonautonomous vehicles.[5]

Connectedness of Autonomous Vehicles

Policymakers and the autonomous-vehicle industry will need to engage constructively to gain a better understanding of the public investments that are needed to facilitate the various communications between vehicles and between vehicles and the street-level infrastructure, the entire road network in a city and region, and possibly pedestrians. As MacDuffie (2018) notes, Google's original plan was to turn autonomous vehicles into independent cells that would not be reliant on direct communications from other vehicles or smart infrastructure. However, others believe that peak safety would be obtained only if V2V or vehicle-to-infrastructure (V2I) communication (or both) were implemented. One approach would be to develop a closed and controlled communications system, similar to air-traffic control. However, critics argue that a single communications system would require too many competing algorithms to be feasible. Clearly, policymakers, automakers, and technology companies must resolve how vehicles will communicate with one another and with the street-level and highway infrastructure.

In 1999 the Federal Communications Commission reserved the wireless 5.9 GHz spectrum band for transportation-communication traffic using dedicated short-range communication, which facilitates both V2V and V2I communication. Technology has improved since then, most notably with cellular vehicle-to-everything (C-V2X) communication, which can offer V2V, V2I, and vehicle-to-pedestrian communication. The C-V2X system is designed to be compatible with the forthcoming 5G mobile technology. However, the Federal Communications Commission has not allowed C-V2X systems to use the 5.9 GHz spectrum. Currently, there is a debate among the automakers about communication systems, with one side favoring the status quo and the other favoring a change based on the system that their vehicle is designed to use. In any case, restrictions on the 5.9 GHz wireless spectrum could stifle the growth and market vitality of more effective 5G-compatible technology.

Notwithstanding federal actions, local and state governments will need to make investments to upgrade the physical characteristics and communication capabilities of their infrastructure to facilitate autonomous-vehicle travel. Duvall and others (2019) depicts a revamped infrastructure for a city that would facilitate and promote autonomous-vehicle operations that includes advanced traffic management, providing routing and pricing information; maintenance, storage, and charging facilities; curb modifications to facilitate flexible pickup and drop-off of passengers and freight; metered pricing for remaining on-street parking; and possibly mobility hubs to integrate multiple modes.

Cities such as Los Angeles have outlined preliminary plans to help introduce autonomous vehicles, and a few regional associations have begun to offer guidance to metropolitan areas about their infrastructure investments to enable travelers to use autonomous vehicles.[6] However, Freemark, Hudson, and Zhao (2019), assessing the autonomous-vehicle preparedness of transportation and planning officials in 120 America cities with populations greater than 100,000, find that only 24 percent have issued strategies for maximizing the possible safety and congestion-easing benefits of autonomous vehicles. Most cities say that they are waiting for higher levels of government to set the rules of the road, which suggests another way that federal delays are slowing the adoption of autonomous vehicles.

City officials must also recognize that traffic signaling and speed limits in urban areas, designed for nonautonomous vehicles, have contributed to hundreds of millions of annual hours of delay because they are based on out-of-date historical data instead of real-time traffic flows (National Transportation Operations Coalition 2007). Local transportation agencies should act immediately to upgrade signage and traffic signals, or possibly replace them with radio transmitters, and base their operations on real-time traffic conditions using GPS technology. Specifically, the duration of traffic signals should be optimized to maximize efficient traffic flow; flashing-red signals should be used at intersections during times of day when they are lightly used; and warning signals should be given to stopped vehicles at intersections of an impending green light to reduce start-up delays, which have a surprisingly large negative effect on travel time. Winston and Mannering (2014) reports estimates that cutting start-up delays in half could reduce the delays caused by signals by nearly 20 percent, with little effect on safety.

Some states are trying to align their infrastructure in advance with autonomous-vehicle technology. For example, Utah's Department of Transportation and Panasonic are developing and testing a system that enables vehicles, roads, and signals to communicate with one another to enhance safety. The goal is to allow cars and road facilities to constantly broadcast information to one another about conditions, location of obstacles, signal timing, and the speed, direction, and position of all cars. The Colorado Department of Transportation's "internet of roads" project is exploring the technologies to facilitate V2V and V2I communication. Michigan's Department of Transportation is working with 3M to provide signage concepts, pavement markings, and work-zone barrels, which include invisible codes that can be read by the sensor-equipped autonomous vehicles for guidance purposes but not by the driver. The California Department of Transportation (Caltrans) is modifying the state's roads by phasing out Botts' dots—round, nonreflective pavement markers that warn drivers that they are drifting out of their lanes—with thicker lane lines that autonomous vehicles can see more easily. And several states are installing fiber-optic lines in roads that can send electronic warnings to autonomous vehicles about hazards ahead and other information to make them more aware of their surroundings. Such engineering improvements indicate that policymakers are aware that the U.S. road system that was built and operated for nonautonomous vehicles must be changed to facilitate autonomous vehicles' operations and that by delaying those changes, they will delay the use of autonomous vehicles on their roads.

To manage the traffic flow over the highway network more efficiently, traffic engineers will have to recalculate the number of vehicles that roads can handle if, as expected, autonomous vehicles can travel safely while reducing the distance between vehicles. Travel times could be optimized with GPS technology by setting variable speed limits that are properly aligned with real-time traffic flows and with other driving conditions, such as weather. Autonomous vehicles could then align their speeds with those limits. Implementing those types of modern technologies to enable traffic signaling and highway speed limits to complement and enhance the operations of autonomous vehicles would realize urban planners' goal of creating "smart roads" that are capable of communicating with autonomous vehicles to improve traffic flows and enhance safety.

Finally, autonomous vehicles may not have to develop direct digital communications with pedestrians, but reckless incidents that have occurred during road tests have raised concerns. In one incident, for example, pedestrians have "attacked" autonomous vehicles and even tried to climb on them. In another, a self-driving Uber vehicle was unable to avoid hitting and killing a pedestrian in Tempe, Arizona, because its emergency brake was disabled and the test driver apparently did not have his hands on the steering wheel just before the accident. Autonomous vehicles will be better at learning from accidents than pedestrians are because once they understand why an unsafe incident occurred, even if it was precipitated by a reckless pedestrian, they develop a solution that can be used by all autonomous vehicles. Pedestrians will have to learn individually how to adapt to autonomous-vehicle technology, which should generally be much less of a threat to their safety than what they encounter with nonautonomous vehicles.

Reforming Pricing and Investment Policies

Autonomous-vehicle operations have the potential, in theory, to significantly reduce congestion by creating a smooth traffic flow, where cars can travel close together without fear of an accident. In practice, autonomous-vehicle operations could be disrupted by congestion that arises from induced demand—that is, the improved travel conditions could attract drivers who previously avoided traveling during peak travel periods—and by damaged pavement that requires vehicles to slow down or take measures to avoid potholes. Autonomous vehicles cannot solve those problems by themselves; efficient policy reforms are required. Enacting those reforms could also help reduce sprawl, vehicle damage, and highway budget deficits.

Congestion Pricing

According to Downs' law (Downs 1962), peak-hour congestion rises to meet maximum road capacity because of latent demand, which is likely to be stimulated by the expanded highway capacity that is created by autonomous vehicles. However, Downs' law would not apply in practice if policymakers set congestion tolls that were adjusted to real-time traffic volumes, because the higher out-of-pocket costs would discourage some travelers from using major thoroughfares even if the travel times for autonomous vehicles were faster and more reliable.

Generally, a highway authority could set real-time congestion tolls by using GPS navigation services to determine traffic volume on a stretch of road during a given time interval and by drawing on plausible congestion-cost estimates available in the empirical literature. Singapore is well-known for its sophisticated congestion-pricing scheme, which varies sharply by location, the extent of congestion, and time of day (Santos 2005). It is planning on introducing a global-navigation-satellite system in 2020 to further improve the accuracy of its road pricing.[7]

In practice, the specific charge for a given trip could be communicated to travelers through a built-in feature of the vehicle. At the beginning of a trip, the autonomous vehicle would offer trip options with predicted times and either predicted or fixed congestion charges. Drivers would then select their preferred option, and the trip would commence. During the trip, the vehicle could offer route changes that would indicate predicted travel-time savings and revised congestion charges. Technologically, it would be possible to set a fixed charge at the beginning of the trip or a variable charge dependent on changes in traffic flows. In the latter case, individuals would make initial decisions based on predicted charges. The fixed-charge system would generate less anger over changing prices and is probably a more sensible option. If such a system were used, then the charge would be based on predicted traffic when the autonomous vehicle reaches a particular street, not on the traffic when the trip began. Allowing travelers to make choices based on observed prices has the advantage of making the congestion charge highly salient, maximizing its impact on reducing driving on the most congested thoroughfares. Currently, modern electronic tolling is less salient than the charging system outlined here, so drivers may be less likely to respond to the cost of driving (Finkelstein 2009).

Policymakers could introduce congestion pricing with the adoption of autonomous vehicles, and there is some congressional support for this action.[8] In addition, efficient road pricing would be more politically palatable in the new driving environment because a notable percentage of people would not own cars and would simply hire an autonomous vehicle when they need transportation. Hence, congestion tolls may be perceived as similar to a toll paid when using a taxi or surge charges paid when using shared transportation, such as Uber or Lyft, and would therefore be more likely to be accepted.

Congestion pricing would reduce the highway congestion caused by the increased demand for autonomous-vehicle travel during peak periods, thereby preserving much of the economic gains that we estimate would result from less congestion and delay. At the same time, our illustration in chapter 2 of the potential gains to travelers from adopting autonomous vehicles would have to include the cost of peak-period congestion tolls along with the other changes in the cost of driving, but possibly no longer owning, a vehicle.

Congestion pricing would also be an attractive way to help finance highway infrastructure in a world of autonomous vehicles. Much of the American expressway network is part of the System of Interstate and Defense Highways, established in the 1950s and built using federal fuel taxes in the decades since. With a few exceptions, Congress has refused to allow the states to toll interstate-system highways, on the grounds that motorists have already paid for them through the fuel tax. This position has become less tenable as highways have aged and needed rehabilitation, the Highway Trust Fund has accumulated deficits because of improvements in vehicle fuel economy, and the federal gasoline tax has been fixed since 1993.

In 2012 federal authorities allowed states to impose tolls on highway segments that were being rebuilt, so long as there was no reduction in the number of untolled general-purpose lanes. It is striking that many of the express-lane projects are financially self-supporting from tolls, despite built-in competition from the free general-purpose lanes (Collier and Goodin 2002). Some generate enough toll revenues to subsidize the reconstruction of the general-purpose lanes as well. The larger projects often involve investments of $2 billion or more and are executed through public-private partnerships, with the private investors financing the construction and operations in return for the revenues on the toll lanes. The advantages are such that several of America's fastest-growing states—Florida, Texas, Minnesota, California, and Colorado—are planning networks of express lanes.

Congestion pricing would also complement the changes in land use attributable to autonomous vehicles. First, it is likely to discourage sprawl and the market failures associated with it by making long-distance commuters pay the social marginal costs of their trips and by eliminating the comparatively larger subsidies that those commuters receive by paying only the gasoline tax (Brueckner 2000). Second, although autonomous vehicles would free up space downtown currently used for parking, some travelers who own autonomous vehicles would continue to park them on city streets. A GPS-based system should therefore be used to impose on those vehicles efficient parking charges that vary with traffic volumes throughout the day (Shoup 2005). By charging travelers efficiently for their vehicles' stationary use of a city street, regulators would encourage them to enroll in subscription transportation services to avoid those charges.

Finally, the combination of congestion pricing and autonomous-vehicle transportation would strengthen the case for eliminating inefficient land-use policies, including zoning, regulations that establish minimum lot sizes, and minimum-parking requirements, which attempt to limit congestion on local streets and excess demand for parking places. In fact, those policies have done little to reduce congestion, even as they have created other costs. Glaeser (2011) and Glaeser and Ward (2009) show that zoning and minimum-lot-size regulations increase housing prices and promote sprawl by reducing residential density; Cutter and Franco (2012) and McDonnell, Madar, and Been (2011) find that minimum-parking requirements have caused an oversupply of parking places and increased housing costs. By eliminating zoning that restricts new housing supply, the aggregate costs of spatial misallocation of labor across U.S. cities could also be reduced (Hsieh and Moretti 2018).

Pavement-Wear Pricing and Optimal Highway Durability

Roads in many urban areas are undermaintained, which will create a particular challenge for autonomous vehicles because early models are likely to have difficulty recognizing and avoiding large potholes. Driving on rough and uneven surfaces can compromise the calibration of LIDAR and cause excessive wear on the ball bearings that stabilize the sensor on top of the vehicle. In that event, the LIDAR sensor would have to be replaced more frequently. As the quality of the LIDAR sensor improves, autonomous vehicles may succeed in avoiding potholes only by significantly disturbing the traffic flow and increasing travel times.

To some extent, autonomous vehicles can help to overcome the challenges of operating in urban areas because one of their key features is the ability to learn from risky driving situations and to reprogram their technology to avoid such situations in the future. Autonomous vehicles could also identify problems in a city's infrastructure that compromise their operations and could report those trouble spots to urban-road authorities. Boston, for example, has an app, called Street Bump, that uses smart phones to automatically report rough roads to city officials. A group of engineering students at MIT, Harvard, and other schools has developed an app that turns a smartphone into a tool to measure overall road quality (for example, the surface streets of Cambridge have the roughness index of a well-maintained dirt road). Such reporting tools could be directly incorporated into autonomous vehicles and could continuously improve local officials' knowledge of the weaknesses in their road systems, which they could use to take constructive action.

However, it will also be important for policymakers to take action to reduce the damage that trucks inflict on road pavements and to keep the pavements durable by instituting pavement-wear charges for trucks and by building road thicknesses to optimal durability. The combination of those policies would help to reduce autonomous vehicles' travel times and repair bills, expenses that currently run in the billions of dollars annually for owners of nonautonomous vehicles (TRIP 2016).

The extent of pavement damage depends on a truck's weight per axle, where the damage caused by an axle is defined in terms of the number of equivalent standard-axle loads (ESALs) causing the same damage; the standard is a single axle of 18,000 pounds. Efficient road pricing encourages truckers to reduce their ESALs or weight per axle whenever possible by shifting to trucks with more axles (or by adding an axle to their truck), thus extending pavement life and reducing highway-maintenance expenditures and vehicle-repair costs. The fuel tax currently in use provides truckers with the opposite, and thus perverse, incentive: the tax rises with a vehicle's axles, since trucks with more axles require larger engines and get lower fuel economy.[9]

Technology is available to implement real-time pavement-wear pricing for autonomous trucks. A highway authority can implement an axle-weight tax by estimating a truck's ESAL miles using high-speed weigh-in-motion technologies. Those technologies use sensors that are installed in one or more traffic lanes to identify a vehicle and record its number of axles, vehicle load, and journey while it continues to travel in the traffic stream. The total charge would then be sent to the truck's owner as the product of the truck's ESAL miles and a plausible estimate of the resurfacing costs per ESAL mile. Empirical studies indicate that replacing the fuel tax with an axle-weight charge would encourage truckers to shift to vehicles with more axles that do less damage to road pavements, thereby reducing the extent and speed of pavements' deterioration (Small, Winston, and Evans 1989).

The damage that a truck does to a pavement depends not only on its axle weight but also on the durability (thickness) of the pavement. Historically, road pavements have been built too thin to accommodate trucks efficiently, especially for heavily traveled urban highways (Small and Winston 1988). Road thickness has not been designed to minimize the sum of initial capital costs and long-run maintenance costs, in all likelihood because all levels of government have placed a priority on completing their road systems with the funds that are available instead of delaying a system's completion by building roads to be more durable. In the long run, governments have incurred a cost for their impatience by spending more money on maintenance than thicker roads would have cost them, and road users have suffered longer travel times and greater damage and repair costs to their vehicles.

Combining efficient axle-weight prices with efficient investments in more durable, thicker pavement would enable the pavement to last much longer and remain in much better condition than pavement on current roads. In addition, charges to truckers would decrease because their vehicles would do less damage to more durable roads, which should soften their opposition to the change in policy. And the package of efficient pricing and investment policies, including congestion charges for cars and trucks, could generate sufficient revenues to enable the U.S. road system to be self-financed (Small, Winston, and Evans 1989).

Finally, given the increase in safety attributable to autonomous cars and trucks and to efficient truck charges and investment policy, which would increase road quality and durability, policymakers could increase trucking productivity and reduce social costs by relaxing truck size and weight limits without jeopardizing safety or accelerating pavement deterioration.[10]

Expanding Highway Capacity

On highways specifically designed for autonomous vehicles, the number and width of highway lanes could be modified, which would expand capacity in two ways. First, autonomous cars and trucks could "communicate" with the autonomous-vehicle infrastructure so that their speed would be immediately and safely governed when they entered their respective lanes. Thus cars and trucks would become part of an algorithm-controlled collective transportation system, organized to optimize traffic flow and eliminate driver error. Given autonomous vehicles' safe and reliable operations, the width of highway lanes could be narrowed, allowing the total number of lanes to be increased even at free-flow speeds.

Second, autonomous vehicles could provide constant real-time safety and fuel inspections and report the results to smart sensors embedded in the highway. Vehicles with significant safety risk or insufficient fuel could receive an electronic message that they would not be allowed to use the autonomous highway, while those that developed trouble during the journey could be rerouted to service centers adjacent to the highway. Safety monitoring of the vehicles would further reduce the risk of accidents and loss of life. Given those operations, the elimination of driver error, and the ongoing replacement of older vehicles with newer, more reliable vehicles, breakdown lanes would become virtually unnecessary and could be eliminated, further expanding the number of available highway lanes.[11]

The improvements in highway design—combined with congestion pricing, which would smooth demand throughout the day—would accommodate much higher travel speeds and greater safety than exists on current roads. The exact upper speed limit is an engineering issue, but 100 miles per hour could be a reasonable expectation—a dramatic improvement in safe mobility compared with current driving conditions in any part of the world with high traffic volumes.

In sum, the symptoms of congestion, delays, and deteriorating infrastructure have been erroneously interpreted by the public as the consequence of policymakers' unwillingness or inability to substantially increase spending on the U.S. road system. However, it should be clear that those symptoms largely reflect the failure of policymakers to implement efficient highway pricing, investment, and technology policies, which do not require a massive increase in highway expenditures. The expenditures that are made, for example, to increase durability would not cost public taxpayers much because they would be funded by efficient user taxes.

In table 9-1, we summarize how those policy reforms would greatly improve travel conditions and would enable autonomous vehicles to generate the large social benefits associated with faster and more reliable travel times and safer operations. The failure to adopt efficient policies in a world of nonautonomous vehicles has been costly; the failure to adopt such policies in a world of autonomous vehicles may entail even greater social costs by preventing a major technological advance from realizing its potential.

Table 9-1

Policy Reforms and their Effects on the Performance of Autonomous Vehicles

Action	Effect on travel conditions
Pricing	
Pavement-wear (axle-weight) pricing of trucks	Reduces pavement damage and disruptions to the traffic flow because of potholes and uneven pavement
Congestion pricing of cars and trucks	Expand highway capacity, which will also offset induced demand that reduces travel time savings from autonomous vehicles
Investment	
Increasing pavement durability	Reduces pavement damage and disruptions to the traffic flow because of potholes and uneven pavement
Increasing number of traffic lanes and eliminate breakdown lane	Expand highway capacity, which will also offset induced demand that reduces travel time savings from autonomous vehicles
Technology adoption	
Optimizing traffic signaling that accounts for real-time traffic flows	Improves traffic flows and travel times
Including a warning signal to reduce start-up delays	Improves traffic flows and travel times
Implementing variable speed limits that account for real-time traffic flows	Improves traffic flows and travel times

Highway Privatization

If the public sector compromises the performance of autonomous vehicles by failing to reform inefficient highway pricing and investment policies and by failing to effectively implement changes in infrastructure technology, privatization of the road system could be considered as an alternative approach to improve the system's efficiency and technology. For example, it has been argued that air-traffic control would be more efficient and technologically up-to-date if it were privatized along the lines of Nav Canada (Robyn 2015).

However, the challenges of privatization are formidable, and, at this point, the effects are uncertain. To begin with, a competitive private-highway market would have to be designed. Winston and Yan (2011) analyzes the economic effects of highway privatization by characterizing a competitive environment on State Route 91 in California consisting of two routes with equal lane capacities that would be operated by two different private highway companies. A third party would represent motorists, negotiating tolls and capacities with the private companies to obtain a contract equilibrium. The authors find that motorists could gain from highway privatization when the contract equilibrium consisted of differentiated prices and service—that is, when motorists were given a choice of paying a high toll to use lanes with little congestion or paying a low toll to use lanes that were highly congested.

In practice, the United States has had little experience with highway privatization. It is uncertain whether policymakers could effectively design a competitive private-highway system and whether sufficient managerial talent exists to operate several competing highway companies that would remain profitable and provide highway services capable of improving motorists' welfare. The privatization option should be explored with carefully designed experiments, which could give policymakers valuable guidance on whether to privatize the entire U.S. highway system and under what conditions.[12] However, policymakers have not shown any interest in conducting highway-privatization experiments with that goal in mind.

We conclude the book by turning back to the public sector, exploring how government could be motivated to overcome its status quo bias, to reform its current policies and implement new policies efficiently to enable autonomous vehicles to significantly benefit the nation.

10

Conclusion

The autonomous vehicle is a life-altering innovation that has the at-tractive feature of both increasing consumption, by improving the nation's GDP growth, employment, and labor earnings, and saving lives (Jones 2016). The successful adoption of autonomous vehicles would be a potential cure for sluggish economic growth and would counter the pessimistic view that the lack of innovation in the future may prevent living standards from improving (Gordon 2016). The World Economic Forum and Intel peg autonomous vehicles' even-tual annual social benefits at several trillion dollars (Schwartz 2018). Our estimate of the annual benefits from reducing congestion—combined with plausible estimates of the benefits from improving health, safety, accessibility, land use, and job creation—suggests a similar order of magnitude.

Historically, the federal government has taken constructive ac-tions to enable its infrastructure to facilitate innovations. During the 1990s, it fostered the success of cell phones, smartphones, and other mobile devices by allocating and auctioning off a large part of the electromagnetic spectrum for use by cellular technology. Fur-ther innovations in mobile devices and location-based services were enabled after the GPS system, developed and operated by the federal government, was opened to civilian applications and higher locational accuracies were made available.

The federal government must also reform its highway-infrastructure policies to unlock the enormous benefits of autonomous vehicles. Unfortunately, its track record in adopting such policies has been poor, despite the pleadings of economists and other analysts, although some local and state officials are taking the lead in upgrading their highway technology to facilitate autonomous-vehicle operations. At the same time, the autonomous-vehicle industry has been frustrated by policymakers' delays in passing legislation to provide a national testing and adoption framework.

However, even if such a framework were developed and the public began to adopt autonomous vehicles, why would policymakers address the policy requirements of autonomous vehicles when they have failed in the past to implement efficient transportation policies for nonautonomous vehicles? Several considerations may induce policymakers to eventually be receptive to implementing efficient highway-policy reforms to align highway infrastructure to a world of autonomous vehicles.

First, competition at the local, state, and international level to offer reliable and efficient autonomous-vehicle transportation will develop and is developing already, as some cities and states have begun to form partnerships with private companies and to make new investments to develop their technology to facilitate autonomous-vehicle operations. Other U.S. localities will not want to be left behind as the leading U.S. cities and states demonstrate the benefits of efficient autonomous-vehicle operations for everyone to see. As noted in chapter 2, Bloomberg has created a website that identifies the cities where autonomous vehicles are being tested. It is also likely that Bloomberg and others will create websites that identify the cities where travelers are able to use autonomous vehicles and the efficiency of those operations.

The United States will also want to maintain its position as the world leader in autonomous technology and will not want to fall behind other countries, especially China, in adopting the technology.[1] The large welfare gains from efficient autonomous-vehicle operations will cause geographic competition to intensify because inefficiencies will be transparent and may become politically costly to policymakers in cities, states, and countries with no or inadequate autonomous-vehicle operations.

Second, widespread adoption of autonomous vehicles is likely to increase the practice of sharing instead of owning vehicles. As a consequence, congestion pricing may become less politically objectionable, because ride-sharing travelers will be accustomed to paying a charge per use. Riders do so today, with Uber and Lyft, and the price of those services often includes additional fees (for example, surge charges or tolls) as part of the full price. The additional charges that account more precisely for congestion would deter excess driving. Yet they are more likely than an explicit congestion tax, observed and paid directly by drivers who own their vehicles, to enjoy public acceptance.

Third, while autonomous and eventually electric vehicles would exacerbate the highway-budget deficit that continues to grow because highway funding relies on the fuel tax, governments could accrue significant additional revenues from congestion charges for cars and trucks and from pavement-wear charges for trucks, which would relieve pressure on policymakers to remedy perennial funding shortfalls and to develop new funding sources. In short, the infrastructure crisis could be solved.[2] Public officials must demonstrate their commitment to improving road performance by using those funds to finance investments to repair and expand roads and to modernize technology for pricing, traffic signaling, and speed limits. As noted, truckers' opposition to pavement-wear charges would soften if some of the revenue from those charges were used to build roads to optimal durability and if truck sizes and weight limits were subsequently increased.

Fourth, the combination of autonomous vehicles and efficient highway policies would greatly expand highway capacity and would mean that Congress could focus its attention on formulating and passing a modest infrastructure-spending program that enhances the performance of autonomous vehicles instead of attempting to pass an enormous general infrastructure-spending program—or pressure the states to fund such a program—which, given current policy inefficiencies, may not significantly improve the performance of the highway system and may actually reduce social welfare (Gallen and Winston 2018). Given the tight labor market, it may also be difficult to find enough new construction workers so that highway rebuilding is completed without major delays. Compensation may have to be raised considerably to draw more workers into the highway construction industry.

Finally, even in a world of autonomous vehicles without efficient policy reforms, the general public would be able to observe on roads with segregated autonomous- and nonautonomous-vehicle traffic that travelers in autonomous vehicles experience faster speeds, and to experience for themselves some improvement in the speed, reliability, and safety of road transportation when they use an autonomous vehicle. Again, the costly failure of policymakers to adopt efficient highway policies may become more transparent because the public may realize that the performance of autonomous vehicles could be even better. If so, political pressure may finally push policymakers to reform highway policies along the lines that we have suggested because their failure to do so would significantly reduce the benefits of a major technological advance and could result in billion-if not trillion-dollar bills being left on the sidewalk.

Appendix

Measuring Freight Flows across Urban Areas

The computation we perform to measure freight flows across urban areas is

$$Flow_{ij}^{UA} = \Sigma_o \Sigma_d Flow_{od}^{C} \times pop_o^i \times pop_d^i, \tag{A-1}$$

where $Flow_{ij}^{UA}$ is the commodity flow from urban area i to urban area j; $Flow_{od}^{C}$ is the commodity flow from county o to county d; pop_o^i is the percentage of county o's urban-area population that falls within urban area i; and pop_d^i is the percentage of county d's urban-area population that falls within urban area j. This computation makes three assumptions:

- freight flows come and go only to and from urban areas in a county

- the share of a county's freight flows that come from and go to a particular urban area is proportional to the share of that county's population that lives in the urban area

- the volume of freight flows entering (or leaving) an urban area is independent of the urban area of origin (or destination)

To illustrate the intuition behind this computation, consider the flow from the Fresno urban area ($Fresno^{UA}$) to the Riverside urban area ($Riverside^{UA}$). $Fresno^{UA}$ is contained in two counties: Fresno County and Madera County. $Riverside^{UA}$ is contained in two counties: Riverside County and San Bernardino County. Suppose that $Fresno^{UA}$ contains 100 percent of Fresno County's urban-area population and 10 percent of Madera County's urban-area population. Further suppose that $Riverside^{UA}$ contains 100 percent of Riverside County's urban population but only 10 percent of San Bernardino County's urban population.

If we (plausibly) suppose that commodity flows across counties are limited to the urban areas of those counties, then 100 percent of Fresno County's freight flows and 10 percent of Madera County's freight flows are generated by $Fresno^{UA}$, whereas 100 percent of Riverside County's freight flows and 10 percent of San Bernardino County's freight flows are generated by $Riverside^{UA}$. Consequently, the probability that one ton of freight flow moving from Fresno County to Riverside County originated from the portion of $Fresno^{UA}$ that lies in Fresno County and arrived at the portion of $Riverside^{UA}$ that lies in Riverside County is equal to 100 percent × 100 percent = 1. Similarly, the probability that one ton of freight flow moving from Fresno County to San Bernardino County originated from the portion of $Fresno^{UA}$ that lies in Fresno County and arrived at the portion of $Riverside^{UA}$ that lies in San Bernardino County is equal to 100 percent × 10 percent = 0.1. Furthermore, the probability that one ton of freight flow moving from Madera County to San Bernardino County originated from the portion of $Fresno^{UA}$ that lies in Madera County and arrived at the portion of $Riverside^{UA}$ that lies in San Bernardino County is equal to 10 percent × 10 percent = 0.01—and so forth. The total flows from $Fresno^{UA}$ to $Riverside^{UA}$ can then be computed by summing the county-level flows that originated in $Fresno^{UA}$ and arrived in $Riverside^{UA}$.

We provide a robustness check by also computing urban-area flows by taking a simple average of county-level flows. That is,

$$\text{AltFlow}_{ij}^{UA} = \Sigma_o \Sigma_d \frac{1}{m_{ij}} \text{Flow}_{od}^{C}, \qquad \text{(A-2)}$$

where m_{ij} is the number of county *OD* (origination-destination) pairs that make up an urban-area *OD* pair. We find that *AltFlow* and *Flow* produced nearly identical results. We therefore present only the results for models that use *Flow* as the dependent variable—that is, that weight flows according to urban-area population size.

Notes

Chapter 1

1. The value of the entire U.S. paved-road network is even greater.

2. Aschauer (1989) and Munnell (1990) provide the initial empirical support for increasing highway-infrastructure spending to spur productivity growth. A heated debate has ensued over the magnitude of the returns from such spending. Shatz and others (2011) and Melo, Graham, and Brage-Ardao (2013) have conducted extensive surveys of the literature and conclude that the returns are context specific and vary greatly.

3. Pigou (1920) presents the pioneering analytical framework of efficient highway pricing and investment. Walters (1961) provides a formal model in a short-run framework, Mohring and Harwitz (1962) recasts the formal analysis into a long-run framework, and Vickrey (1963) outlines how efficient road pricing could be implemented in practice. Small, Winston, and Evans (1989) expands the framework for analyzing heavy trucks along with cars. Winston (1991), Small and Verhoef (2007), and Winston (2013) survey the empirical evidence that documents the inefficiencies attributable to highway pricing and investment policy in practice.

4. Edwards (2018) points out that the average state diverts 24 percent of its fuel-tax revenue to nonhighway activities.

5. In addition, the Pentagon, which through the Defense Advanced Research Projects Agency had been funding research into self-driving vehicles for years and which sponsored its first competition in 2004, became interested in developing and deploying autonomous tanks on the battlefield and trucks to deliver food, fuel, and other logistics to soldiers engaged in combat.

6. Major automobile companies: BMW, Daimler, Fiat-Chrysler, Ford, General Motors (Cruise), Honda, Hyundai, Renault-Nissan, Toyota, Volkswagen, and Volvo. Cargo companies: Marble, Nuro, and Starship. Technology companies: Alphabet (Waymo), Apple, Aptiv, Baidu, Didi Chuxing, Tesla, and Uber. Start-up companies: Argo.ai, Aeva, Aurora, Embark, Navya, Oxbotica, Pony.ai, Roadstar.ai, TuSimple, and Zoox. Alphabet (Waymo), Apple, Daimler, Embark, Tesla, TuSimple, Uber, and Volvo are also developing autonomous trucking services.

7. As a recent example of a university industry partnership, MIT researchers (in a project backed by the Toyota Research Institute) have created a system that uses minute changes in shadows to predict whether or not an autonomous vehicle can expect a moving object, including pedestrians, cyclists, and other vehicles on the road, to come around a corner. Darrell Etherington, "MIT Uses Shadows to Help Autonomous Vehicles See around Corners," Tech Crunch, October 28, 2019, https://techcrunch .com/2019/10/28/mit-uses-shadows-to-help-autonomous-vehicles-see-around-corners/.

8. Hyunjoo Jin, "Hyundai Motor Group to Invest $35 Billion in Future Automotive Tech," Reuters, October 15, 2019, https://www.reuters.com/article /southkorea-hyundai-motor/hyundai-motor-group-to-invest-35-billion-in-future-automotive-tech-idUSL3N2701BZ.

9. See, for example, LaReau (2019) and Howard and Greg Gardner (2017). Ford has more recently announced that it plans to begin production of self-driving vehicles in 2021 at a production center in Michigan.

10. As a further point, the alleged justification for the U.S. government's bailout of Chrysler and General Motors during the Great Recession was that their collapse could bring down the U.S. manufacturing sector, which could turn the recession into a depression. The failure of autonomous vehicle companies, including automobile manufacturers and technology firms, to succeed in the United States could also have devastating

implications for the U.S. economy. Critics of the technology do not consider the implications of their predictions and they do not offer constructive warnings to policymakers. We do not believe that such warnings are necessary.

11. Policymakers could also pursue poor trade policies that slow the development of autonomous vehicles by inhibiting shared technology between firms from different countries. For example, a U.S. self-driving software developer, Plus.ai, has recently teamed up with a Chinese truck maker, FAW, but its exports and thus funding could be curtailed by proposed export controls. Overall, Chinese firms are expected to provide billions of dollars in funding for U.S. firms in the coming years that could be in jeopardy.

Chapter 2

1. Darrell Etherington, "Over 1,400 Self-Driving Vehicles Are Now in Testing by 80+ Companies across the U.S.," Tech Crunch, June 11, 2019, https://techcrunch.com/2019/06/11/over-1400-self-driving-vehicles-are-now-in-testing-by-80-companies-across-the-u-s/.

2. "Predicting Pedestrian Movement in 3D for Driverless Cars," Michigan Engineering YouTube channel (video), February 15, 2019, www.youtube.com/watch?v=YIB8IALSwmE.

3. Matthew Doude, Christopher Goodin, and Daniel Carruth, "Driving Autonomous Cars Off the Beaten Path," The Conversation, November 8, 2018, http://theconversation.com/driving-autonomous-cars-off-the-beaten-path-105925.

4. The companies are Aptiv, Audi, Baidu, BMW, Continental, Daimler, Fiat Chrysler, Infineon Intel, and Volkswagen. The framework is contained in the whitepaper "Safety First for Automated Driving," published in 2019 (https://www.daimler.com/documents/innovation/other/safety-first-for-automated-driving.pdf).

5. "Critical Reasons for Crashes Investigated in the National Motor Vehicle Crash Causation Survey," U.S. Department of Transportation, National Highway Traffic Safety Administration, February 2015, https://crashstats.nhtsa.dot.gov/Api/Public/ViewPublication/812115.

6. Incident delays account for roughly one-third of all delays. Thus, by virtually eliminating accidents, autonomous vehicles can significantly

reduce delays and improve travel time and travel time reliability. Small, Winston, and Yan (2005) finds that motorists' value of more reliable travel times is comparable to their value of reduced travel times.

7. To cut costs, the U.S. postal service is testing self-driving trucks that are supplied by the autonomous trucking firm, TuSimple.

8. A video produced by CDM Smith that shows the evolution of a household's urban transportation from owning vehicles to using shared vehicles to reduce their travel costs ("How Will Driverless Vehicles Change the Way We Travel?") is found at https://www.cdmsmith.com/en/Video/ How-Will-Driverless-Vehicles-Change-the-Way-We-Travel.

9. TaaS could also potentially be provided by taxi companies, car-rental companies, and large employers including government agencies. Autonomous vehicles can also operate as AutoBots with one passenger at a time or TaxiBots with shared rides (International Transport Forum 2015).

10. Auto and technology companies' unwavering interest in a subscription model suggests that the preceding comparison is unlikely to be affected much if we account for industry earnings that they derive from sales of vehicle parts or from other services that they currently provide.

11. Induced travel is caused by an action, such as adopting the use of an autonomous vehicle, that reduces congestion people avoided on a given road by taking alternative less-congested routes, other modes of travel, and so on.

12. Currently, the standards make no reference to autonomous vehicle software. The Department of Transportation has promulgated nonprescriptive and voluntary guidelines for autonomous vehicles. *Automated Vehicles 4.0: Ensuring American Leadership in Automated Vehicle Technologies* (U.S. Department of Transportation [2020]) is the most recent guidance on driverless car development. The Department of Transportation is aiming to craft a unified policy approach for the thirty-eight federal agencies, commissions, and White House offices that have some hand in dealing with the technology. The guidelines seek to avoid rules that would hamper artificial intelligence innovation and growth. *On the Road to Fully Self-Driving* (Waymo 2017) was the first submission by an autonomous vehicle company to the Department of Transportation. It provides a responsive safety evaluation of its autonomous vehicles and a detailed set of protocols for how those vehicles would respond to and avoid colli-

sions. Ford's submission, *A Matter of Trust: Ford's Approach to Developing Self-Driving Vehicles* (Ford Motor Company 2018), indicates that the company hopes to educate the public about how autonomous vehicles could be integrated into society without causing unnecessary risks.

13. The Teamsters, who fear that autonomous vehicles will create unemployment among truck drivers, have thus far been successful at preventing vehicles weighing more than 10,000 pounds from being included in autonomous-vehicle legislation. Thus Congress must work on separate autonomous-truck legislation, which would guide the development and widespread adoption of autonomous motor carriers.

14. As an order of magnitude check, it would take roughly eighteen years to replace the entire vehicle stock in the United States in terms of production, but product adoption is likely to be faster because it tends to follow a sigmoid curve.

15. City governments control the test sites and streets but not the regulations surrounding the development and deployment of autonomous vehicles. The delay in federal regulations suggests that policymakers may be content to focus on getting the technology tested on different streets throughout the country. Arizona has moved aggressively as a testing ground, with Chandler permitting Waymo to test its fully autonomous vehicles with no safety driver. Arlington, Texas, is testing an autonomous shuttle on roads that are closed to other traffic. Bloomberg has developed an up-to-date atlas identifying the cities in the United States and around the globe that are hosting tests of autonomous vehicles, or that have committed to doing so in the near future. (Initiative on Cities and Autonomous Vehicles (webpage), https://avsincities.bloomberg.org).

16. Tesla is challenging the federal government's role in the adoption of autonomous vehicles by promising to make fully self-driving vehicles available to consumers and by claiming that consumers could operate them in the fully autonomous mode. However, we believe that if motorists operate Tesla vehicles in the fully autonomous mode for their personal travel, they will encounter resistance from traffic enforcement and regulators, with the matter going to court. We also believe that the outcome of the legal proceeding would be that motorists are prohibited from operating Tesla vehicles in the fully autonomous mode until the federal government approves the commercial sale and use of autonomous vehicles on the

nation's roads. It could be argued that if fully autonomous Tesla vehicles are as safe as or even safer than nonautonomous vehicles, motorists should be allowed to use them and that their experience could be an informative experiment. Although that is a reasonable argument, we doubt that government officials would be sympathetic to it, and we expect they would unequivocally oppose allowing motorists who are not explicitly authorized to test autonomous vehicles to use them for their personal travel or to let other individuals use them for nontesting purposes.

Chapter 3

1. We report results for a given year, but this is a steady-state result.

2. The order of magnitude of our estimate of the effect of autonomous vehicles on U.S. GDP is consistent with forecasts of the effect of autonomous vehicles on the European (EU-28) economy (Ranft and others 2016).

Chapter 4

1. Istrate, Nowakowski, and Mak (2014) discusses county funding of transportation. The authors point out that counties are increasingly using local-option sales taxes to fund transportation projects, if those taxes are permitted under state law. As of this writing, county residents in fifteen states, including California, have voted for local-option sales taxes for road projects.

2. Keith Dunn, private phone conversation with authors, May 16, 2017.

3. The costs are shown in the conventional diagram to analyze congestion (Lindsey 2006, Winston and Mannering 2014). Langer and Winston (2008) extends the framework to account for congestion's effect on land use and residential location decisions.

4. We also perform estimations using county-level data, discussed later.

5. Although it could be argued from a policy perspective that TTI's benchmark of free-flow speeds is unlikely to be obtained during peak periods, TTI still offers a valid measure of delays caused by traffic congestion, and there is no clear alternative measure. The introduction of autonomous vehicles does offer the possibility of much higher speeds during peak periods.

6. The Moody's Analytics source for employment and wage data is the Bureau of Labor Statistics, "Current Employment Statistics, Quarterly

Census of Employment and Wages," and its source for GDP data is the Bureau of Economic Analysis.

7. We are grateful to Andre Tok and Stephen Ritchie for providing these data. Details on the design and development of the California Statewide Freight Forecasting Model are contained in Ranaiefar (2014) and Ranaiefar and others (2012).

8. Note that $\ln\left(\frac{DV_{t+1}}{DV_t}\right) = \ln\left(1 + \frac{DV_{t+1}-DV_t}{DV_t}\right) \approx \frac{DV_{t+1}-DV_t}{DV_t}$ when $\frac{DV_{t+1}-DV_t}{DV_t}$ is small.

9. However, California counties did not tend to allocate a notable share of the sales taxes to highways until the 1980s.

10. The delays to road projects caused by federal permits and reviews under the National Environment and Policy Act of 1969 have grown considerably over time, and they reportedly average close to ten years (Harrison 2017). We are not aware of efforts to systematically measure the delays to California county road projects caused by California's permitting and environmental standards, but discussions with Caltrans personnel indicate that they average several years.

11. We are grateful to Amber Crabbe for providing the data.

12. Notably, some counties—such as Sonoma—have passed a transportation tax rate other than 0.5 percent, but those counties do not have measurable congestion, so their tax rates do not appear in our table.

13. California's 1971 Transportation Development Act allows any California county to impose a 0.25 percent sales tax, subject to voter approval, for transportation purposes. Subsequently, Sonoma County passed a self-help transportation tax rate of 0.25 percent.

14. Returning to the example of Fresno County, the revenue raised by Fresno's self-help tax may vary from year to year, reflecting changes in consumer spending habits or the strength of the economy. However, the annual share of that revenue going to highways (74 percent) remains constant, reflecting only the initial (and, we argue, exogenous) decision to allocate self-help funds among various transportation projects.

15. Successfully renewing a self-help county tax, especially if expenditure plans change, is still strongly influenced by exogenous political forces.

16. Huet-Vaughn (2019) argues that signage that identified infrastructure projects that were funded by the American Recovery and Reinvestment Act served as a salience mechanism. The process to gain a large share

of voter approval is likely to serve as a salience mechanism for road projects that are funded by self-help county tax expenditures.

17. This information was provided by Norman Hom, executive director of the Sacramento Transportation Authority, in a phone interview with the authors on May 9, 2017.

18. The small impact would also account for any possible increase in employment at the California Department of Transportation to complete highway projects that are included in the self-help tax legislation.

19. We are not aware of empirical evidence that shows the effect of additional spending on California local and state roads on their traffic volume. Diverting travelers from public transit might be a source of greater traffic volume, but that is unlikely to occur in most of the California counties in our sample. Duranton and Turner (2011) reports evidence that Downs' law tends to reflect traffic creation rather than traffic diversion on major roads in their cross section of U.S. cities, but it is likely that the spending that expanded those roads' capacity is notably greater than the spending funded by self-help county taxes. In addition, the spending on major roads that increased their capacity may have been accompanied by additional spending that increased the capacity of freeways, which would contribute to induced demand.

20. Voting records for Sonoma show that earlier self-help county ballots—which proposed a variety of different tax rates—did not result in dramatically different voting outcomes. This suggests that Sonoma's 0.25 percent tax rate is not a response to an extreme antitax environment.

21. Because we do not have pre-1982 congestion data, we define the first self-help tax as the earliest that passed since 1982. For example, Alameda County passed a transportation sales tax in 1969, 1986, and 2000. For this analysis, we define Alameda's first self-help measure as the one that passed in 1986.

22. Furthermore, the Bureau of Economic Analysis provides MSA-level GDP data for the years 2001–2013, which would force us to drop all the years in the sample from the early 1980s to 2000.

23. Note that, for each urban area j, $\Sigma_{i=1}^{N_j} P_{ij} = 1$.

24. According to the California Freight Mobility Plan, the state's intrastate freight flows in 2012 accounted for roughly 77 percent, based on tonnage, of all freight flows transported by truck in California, including

freight to and from other states and to and from other countries (Brown, Kelly, and Dougherty 2014).

25. Put differently, we drop all years in which none of an urban area's counties had voted on (or previously voted on) a countywide transportation sales tax. By limiting our sample to the years in which counties had already demonstrated an interest in self-help county taxes, we hold more unobservables (that is, any correlations between the economy and the political interest in a county self-help tax) constant.

26. The sample size was reduced from 360 urban-area-years to 348 urban-area-years because the dependent variable in our models is an annual growth rate and because we do not observe 2011 annual growth rates. Moreover, two of the California urban areas in the TTI data set do not overlap with a county that has passed a local transportation tax, which further reduced our sample size to 290 urban-area-years. Finally, because the year in which a local transportation tax measure was first voted on varied across counties, different urban areas contributed different numbers of years to our estimation sample, resulting in an unbalanced panel data set of 256 observations.

27. Data that detail self-help county expenditures over time on specific projects were not available.

Chapter 5

1. The Federal Highway Administration estimates that work zones accounted for nearly 900 million person-hours of traveler delay in 2014 (Work Zone Management Program 2016).

2. A quadratic specification broadly captures the importance of accumulating revenues and the delays in reducing congestion. Those effects could not be captured more precisely with a distributed lag model.

3. Any changes in public policies that may affect delay, such as an increase in speed limits, are captured by the year fixed effects.

4. It is possible that a self-help tax in a given county may have spillover effects that improve traffic flows on local and state roads between two counties that did not pass self-help taxes because traffic between those counties goes through the county that passed a self-help tax. However, we are unable to measure that possible effect with our data. We also cannot measure the effect of eliminating a bottleneck that causes congestion to shift upstream or downstream so that total travel time does not fall.

5. We obtain this result by calculating when highway congestion peaks—that is, by setting the derivative of our first-stage regression with respect to the cumulative percentage of self-help taxes spent on highways to zero and then solving for the cumulative percentage of self-help taxes spent on highways. We find that congestion peaked when the cumulative percentage of self-help taxes spent on highways reached 6.99 percent, after which congestion fell.

6. Note, again, that this 34 percent corresponds to the average share of the self-help funds going to highway projects. A much smaller share of the local sales tax base goes to self-help highway projects, as shown in table 4-2.

7. Downs's law could apply, and congestion could eventually revert to its previous level in the long run if there were sufficient induced demand.

8. For example, we explored alternative specifications based on discrete changes and lags in county self-help tax expenditures. Generally, those alternative measures of self-help revenue spending were not significantly correlated with congestion levels. However, when we simply counted the number of years since an urban area began dedicating self-help tax funds toward highway projects and used that variable and its square as instruments in the regression, we found an inverse-U-shaped relation between congestion and the years since an urban area began spending self-help revenue on highways. Using this specification, we also obtained roughly the same 2SLS results, discussed below, that we obtained with the cumulative revenue measures.

9. Table 5-1 reports a statistically significant F statistic and an adjusted R squared = 0.93.

10. The preceding argument also suggests that the possible migration of capital and labor is likely to have little effect on our findings.

11. Any changes in public policies that may affect the performance measures, such as an increase in the minimum wage, are captured by the year fixed effects.

12. Kiron Chatterjee, "Commuting and Wellbeing," University of the West of England, February 2016, https://www1.uwe.ac.uk/et/research/cts/researchprojectsbytheme/influencingbehaviours/commutingandwellbeing.aspx.

13. First, the start dates for self-help taxes seem to be in either the 1984–1990 or the 2004–2008 time frame, both of which include strong

periods of growth. Thus we replace the year dummies with a single time dummy, where 1 indicates a year in the time frame (1984–1990, 2004–2008) and 0 otherwise; we interact this time dummy with the urban-area dummies. Thus our model controls for urban-area-specific average growth rates across the years (1984–1990, 2004–2008). Under this new specification, the congestion effects become stronger, if anything, and retain their statistical significance. Second, we include interactions between the urban-area dummies and an indicator for the time period (2007, 2008) to capture urban-area-specific effects of the Great Recession. We also include individual-year dummies for 2007 and 2008. The congestion effects generally remain economically and statistically significant for this specification. It is likely that different urban areas may have been affected at different times and for different time periods by the Great Recession, but we have no systematic way of specifying time dummies and interacting them with the urban-area dummies to capture that possibility.

14. Our results were robust to interacting a time dummy for the years 1989 and 1990 with our urban-area indicators.

15. Formally, the two steps we take to estimate the model are

Step 1: First-order differencing. Let Δ denote the first-order difference operator, and we have

$$\Delta G_{it} = \alpha \times \Delta C_{it} + \Delta \mathbf{X}_{it}\mathbf{B} + \phi + \theta_i + \Delta \varepsilon_{it}.$$

Step 2: Demeaning. The remaining individual effects can be further removed by demeaning

$$\Delta G_{it} - \Delta \bar{G}_i = \alpha(\Delta C_{it} - \Delta \bar{C}_i) + (\Delta \mathbf{X}_{it} - \Delta \bar{\mathbf{X}}_i)\mathbf{B} + (\Delta \varepsilon_{it} - \Delta \bar{\varepsilon}_i),$$

where $\Delta \bar{G}_i = \frac{1}{R-1} \sum_{t=1}^{R-1} \Delta G_{it}$ and R denotes the number of years in the panel data; $\Delta \bar{\mathbf{X}}_i$, $\Delta \bar{C}_i$, and $\Delta \bar{\varepsilon}_i$ are defined in the same way. Thus the equation is free of individual time trends and individual effects so that the remaining parameters can be consistently estimated by 2SLS using the self-help tax as the instrumental variable.

16. Using the random time-trend effects specification, the estimated coefficient (robust standard error) of the effect of highway congestion on GDP, job, and wage growth was -0.047 (0.025), -0.020 (0.014), and -0.044 (0.027), respectively.

Chapter 6

1. Fagnant and Kockelman (2015) draws on several studies and highway-engineering considerations to quantify the effects of autonomous vehicles on congestion, including smoothed traffic flow and bottleneck reductions, far fewer crashes and incident delays, better routing choices, and further capacity enhancements. The authors acknowledge and account for the possibility that such improvements could be offset to some extent by additional travel induced by autonomous vehicles. Milakis and others (2017) provides a set of projections for the Netherlands and stresses the importance of penetration rates and the positive impact that autonomous vehicles are likely to have on mobility.

2. It is possible that greater scheduling flexibility would lead to more carpooling and thus reduce traffic volumes, but there are still other constraints that may limit the amount of carpooling.

3. As noted, Moody's Analytics uses data from the Bureau of Labor Statistics to determine wages. To obtain consistent estimates for our counterfactuals for California and the nation, we used Bureau of Economic Analysis estimates of earnings by workplace, a category composed of personal income wages and salaries, supplements to wages and salaries, and proprietors' income.

4. We converted thousands of tons of freight commodities into dollar amounts using the average price of a ton of goods trucked in California in 2007, according to the Freight Analysis Framework Data Tabulation Tool (http://faf.ornl.gov/fafweb/Extraction1.aspx). We then summed the total value of freight movements across origin-destination pairs that started and ended in a California county and computed the total intra-California freight-flow values for 2007 and 2010. Using those two data points, we calculated an annual growth rate in freight-flow value between 2007 and 2010 and used that growth rate to impute an "actual" commodity-flow value for 2008. We then performed the rest of the simulation using the procedure outlined above.

5. We cannot include estimates of the effects of autonomous vehicles on the growth rate of U.S. commodity flows owing to the absence of data on commodity flows across U.S. urban areas. Note that actual growth rates and levels are also from the Bureau of Economic Analysis.

6. Our estimates of the effect of autonomous vehicles on GNP are

aligned with Ranft and others (2016), which forecasts the effect of autonomous vehicles on the European (EU-28) economy.

7. Recall that of all the measures of performance, commodity-freight flows had the largest elasticity with respect to highway congestion.

8. Other countries' economies also have the potential to benefit significantly from the adoption of autonomous vehicles. Gill and others (2015) provides an overview of the benefits of autonomous vehicles for the Canadian economy.

9. Nick Szabo, "Transportation, Divergence, and the Industrial Revolution," *Unenumerated* (blog), October 16, 2014, https://unenumerated.blog spot.com/2014/10/transportation-divergence-and.html.

Chapter 7

1. In all likelihood, the adoption of autonomous vehicles will cause insurance coverage to devolve from drivers to vehicle manufacturers and the licensers of software that drives autonomous vehicles.

2. A concern is that autonomous vehicles may become a new way to facilitate prostitution and the use of illegal drugs. Effective police work would be the socially desirable way to address those crimes instead of possibly violating privacy rights or restricting the use of autonomous vehicles for cruising.

3. A case study of New Orleans transit is illustrative. Snyder (2018) reports that in the aftermath of Hurricane Katrina, federal efforts to improve transportation failed to actually connect workers to jobs. Although the average New Orleans resident could reach 89 percent of area jobs by car with a standard half-hour commute, only 12 percent of the area's jobs were accessible by public transit in that time.

4. "Census Bureau Releases Comprehensive Analysis of Fast-Growing 90-and-Older Population," U.S. Census Bureau, November 17, 2011, https://www.census.gov/newsroom/releases/archives/aging_population/cb11-194.html.

5. According to some estimates, there are three nonresidential parking spaces for every car in the United States, and the area per car exceeds the area of housing per person (Dizikes 2012; Shoup 2018).

6. Zakharenko (2016) provides a theoretical analysis of how autonomous vehicles will change urban forms that is consistent with this discussion.

7. Refueling and charging stations to accommodate autonomous and electric vehicles would have to be developed. Kazi and others (2018) characterizes optimal scheduling operations of a station to provide refueling and charging services for those vehicles.

8. Gregg Ip, "Workers: Fear Not the Robot Apocalypse," *Wall Street Journal*, September 5, 2017, https://www.wsj.com/articles/workers-fear-not -the-robot-apocalypse-1504631505.

9. U.S. Bureau of Labor Statistics, "Labor Force Participation Rates Projected to Decline over the Next Decade," *The Economics Daily* (blog), November 01, 2017, https://www.bls.gov/opub/ted/2017/labor-force-partici pation-rates-projected-to-decline-in-the-coming-decade.htm.

10. Keeping trucks moving will have another benefit because forced stops increase the risk of harmful bacteria multiplying in, for example, lettuce.

11. Deliveries within cities may be difficult to fully automate because people may be needed to carry packages to doorsteps and mailboxes and perhaps to obtain signatures from the recipients. In the long run, however, drones may eliminate those jobs.

12. SAFE (2018) outlines various scenarios about the effects of autonomous vehicles on the U.S. labor market. All of them indicate that the benefits of autonomous vehicles greatly outweigh their job-dislocation effects.

13. In December 2019, the first-ever known cross-country commercial freight delivery made by an autonomous truck was completed.

14. The recent transit experience in Los Angeles suggests why transit subsidies are likely to continue to grow. From 2013 to 2018, bus ridership declined 24 percent and rail ridership declined 5 percent. Yet LA Metro is in the midst of a forty-year, $120 billion expansion project, funded by a sales-tax increase in 2016.

15. It is possible that autonomous vehicles may not overwhelm the New York City transit system, given its extensive network of rail track and tunnels. City officials will undoubtedly explore how automation could improve the system's operations and finances. It is also unlikely that, in the foreseeable future, public transit will disappear from cities such as London, Paris, Hong Kong, and the like.

16. See the video and discussion of flying cars, "Google's Larry Page Has Backed two Flying-Car Start-ups—Here's a Look inside One of Them,

Opener," Jillian D'Onfro, CNBC, October 12, 2018, https://www.cnbc
.com/2018/10/12/google-co-founder-larry-page-backs-flying-car-start-up-
opener.html.

17. U.S. Department of Transportation, "Guidance on Treatment of
the Economic Value of a Statistical Life (VSL) in the U.S. Department of
Transportation Analyses—2016 Adjustment" (memo), Office of the Secretary of Transportation, August 8, 2016, https://www.careforcrashvictims
.com/wp-content/uploads/2017/01/2016RevisedValueofaStatisticalLife
Guidance.pdf.

Chapter 8

1. In fact, Waymo has initiated an effort to soften the severity of an
injury in the event that an autonomous vehicle hits a pedestrian by developing a process that uses cables so that the point of impact on the car will
loosen itself structurally to minimize impact. Aurora, which was founded
to develop self-driving technology, outlines the procedures and precau-
tions that it takes to test its vehicles, including conditions under which
it will "ground the fleet," in their report *The New Era of Mobility*, https://
downloads.ctfassets.net/v3j0gnq3qxwi/4QVMTwpB02ZOmE03B09UP2/
611de2c139aef05d7204ace06e946e00/VSSA_Final.pdf.

2. Insurance Institute for Highway Safety (IIHS) and Highway Loss
Data Institute (HLDI), "Lane Departure Warning, Blind Spot Detection
Help Drivers Avoid Trouble," IIHS/HLDI, August 23, 2017, http://www
.iihs.org/iihs/news/desktopnews/stay-within-the-lines-lane-departure-
warning-blind-spot-detection-help-drivers-avoid-trouble. Some have suggested that the adoption of autonomous-vehicle safety features in recent
years may account for the decline in auto fatalities although vehicle miles
traveled have increased, but there is no causal evidence to support this
claim.

3. Light detection and ranging could be blinded by a strong light of
the same wavelength that LIDAR uses to erase the existing objects in the
sensed output of the LIDAR.

4. The autonomous land-driven vehicle project achieved the first road-
following demonstration in the United States. Recently, Tesla has become
an outlier in the autonomous-vehicle industry because it appears to be fo-
cused on getting consumers into their vehicles in the fully autonomous

mode as soon as possible. Tesla's promotion of its fully autonomous operations may be premature, and Tesla could harm the reputation of autonomous vehicles among the public and the policy community if their vehicles are involved in accidents for which their vehicle's technology is deemed to be at fault. As noted, policymakers may play an important role in preventing this possibility from occurring by mounting legal challenges in court to drivers' operation of Tesla vehicles in the fully autonomous mode for any personal or other travel outside of development and testing.

Chapter 9

1. General Motors submitted a request to NHTSA for exemptions for its fully autonomous vehicle to be able to drive on U.S. roads. The agency made GM wait more than fourteen months before it issued a sixty-day public comment period over the proposition. Such delays appear to be inexcusable.

2. Lamotte, de Palma, and Geroliminis (2017) analyzes a variant of the Vickrey (1969) bottleneck model in which autonomous vehicles and conventional vehicles are segregated on different parts of the road network. Autonomous vehicles are subject to central or cooperative control so that their departure rate can be restricted to the relevant bottleneck capacity, avoiding queuing congestion. The paper explores the increase in social surplus that could result from cooperative control of the autonomous-vehicle fleet.

3. Holguin-Veras and others (2003) and California Department of Transportation (2019) discuss truck-only toll lanes or toll roads, which could set a precedent for dedicating space to autonomous trucks on a user-pay basis.

4. State Route 91 in Southern California, for example, contains dedicated toll lanes that have been subject to considerable study by transportation researchers.

5. Optimus Ride, a Boston-based company, is running autonomous shuttles on private roads that transport passengers from the New York City Ferry stop at Dock 72 to Yards' Cumberland Gate at Flushing Avenue. It also has plans to launch autonomous shuttle service at a Fairfield, California, retirement community, a mixed-use development in Reston, Virginia, and an industrial park in Boston's Seaport District. Other cities through-

out the country are also hosting autonomous shuttle demonstrations. As pointed out in the introduction, the coronavirus has spurred demand for autonomous delivery services in China because the small vans help medical providers and consumers reduce human contact and address labor shortages caused by quarantines.

6. Los Angeles's Urban Mobility in a Digital Age plan includes ideas about dedicated lanes for autonomous vehicles, municipal fleets of robotic buses and shuttles, and vehicle data-sharing relationships to help the city manage traffic flow. The Regional Plan Association (2017) offers guidance for investments in autonomous-vehicle infrastructure in the New York metropolitan area.

7. Lehe (2019) provides a recent review of urban-congestion-pricing schemes.

8. For example, Representative Earl Blumenauer (2016), of Oregon's Third Congressional District, argues that the data collection, reporting, and debiting that would be standard in autonomous vehicles could provide a payment platform that could be used to charge for driving during peak travel times. In addition, several states are currently considering a vehicle-miles-traveled tax that could be designed to include a charge for congestion and emissions (Langer, Maheshri, and Winston 2017). Simoni and others (2018) simulates different strategies for implementing congestion pricing for autonomous vehicles, a practice that would reduce congestion but would have various welfare impacts, and Ostrovsky and Schwarz (2018) analyzes road pricing for autonomous vehicles that are used for carpooling.

9. Conventional tolls based on numbers of axles have similar perverse effects.

10. As illustrative evidence, McKinnon (2005) estimates for the United Kingdom that increasing maximum truck weight by 6,700 pounds (a modest 7.3 percent increase over the previous weight limit) resulted in trucking-industry annual operating-cost savings of nearly $250 million (in 2013 dollars) and significant reductions in vehicle miles traveled, congestion, and greenhouse-gas emissions.

11. During the 1980s, engineers tried to cope with traffic on the Brent Spence Bridge, which connects Cincinnati to northern Kentucky, by eliminating the bridge's shoulder lanes and reducing the width of existing

lanes. However, those changes increased accidents and the lengthy delays associated with them. This outcome would not occur with autonomous vehicles, because they would be able to operate safely on narrower lanes.

12. Foreign experience may also be instructive. For example, the vast majority of roads in Sweden and Finland are operated by the private sector and are maintained by local communities. Government works in conjunction with road owners to subsidize the costs of repair and maintenance.

Chapter 10

1. KPMG International suggests that the United States is an effective international competitor in autonomous-vehicle technology and innovation but that its public policy and infrastructure are harming its international competitiveness. Specifically, KPMG looked at the preparation currently in place in 25 major nations for handling the promise and challenges of autonomous vehicles. Their report ranked the United States fourth overall and third in technology and innovation, but ninth in policy and eighth in infrastructure (KPMG International, *2019 Autonomous Vehicles Readiness Index,* https://assets.kpmg/content/dam/kpmg/xx/pdf/2019/02/2019-autonomous-vehicles-readiness-index.pdf).

2. Indeed, policymakers approved congestion pricing in New York City in large part to address a public-finance problem; namely, a significant portion of the toll revenues that are raised will be used to improve the city's cash-strapped transit system. Given the system's vast operating and production inefficiencies (Winston 2019), whether that is an efficient use of the toll revenues is a controversial issue. In any case, New York City appears to be the first city in the United States to adopt congestion pricing, and New York's experience may spur other major cities across the country to do the same.

References

Acemoglu, Daron, and Pascual Restrepo. 2019. "Automation and New Tasks: How Technology Displaces and Reinstates Labor." *Journal of Economic Perspectives* 33 (Spring), pp. 3–30.

Adler, Martin, Stefanie Peer, and Tanja Sinozic. 2018. "Autonomous, Connected, Electric Shared Vehicles (ACES) and Public Finance: An Explorative Analysis." Discussion Paper 19-005/VIII (Amsterdam: Tinbergen Institute), November.

Agrawal, David. 2015. "The Tax Gradient: Spatial Aspects of Fiscal Competition." *American Economic Journal: Economic Policy* 7 (May), pp. 1–29.

Albouy, David, and Bryan Stuart. 2016. "Urban Population and Amenities: The Neoclassical Model of Location." Working Paper 19919 (Cambridge, Mass.: National Bureau of Economic Research), February.

Allen, Treb, and Costas Arkolakis. 2014. "Trade and the Topography of the Spatial Economy." *Quarterly Journal of Economics* 129 (May), pp. 1085–40.

Amiti, Mary, Tyler Bodine-Smith, Michele Cavallo, and Logan T. Lewis. 2015. "Did the West Coast Port Dispute Contribute to the First-Quarter GDP Slowdown?" *Liberty Street Economics* (Federal Reserve Bank of New York), July 2.

Anderson, James E., and Erik van Wincoop. 2004. "Trade Costs." *Journal of Economic Literature* 42 (September), pp. 691–751.

Angel, Shlomo, and Alejandro Blei. 2015. "Commuting and the Productivity of American Cities." Working Paper 19 (New York: New York University, Marron Institute of Urban Management), January 7.

Arieff, Allison. 2019. "Cars Are Death Machines. Self-Driving Tech Won't Change That." *New York Times*, October 4.

Aschauer, David Alan. 1989. "Is Public Expenditure Productive?" *Journal of Monetary Economics* 23 (March), pp. 177–200.

Atkinson, Robert D., and Caleb Foote. 2018. "How the Shift to IT-Enabled Vehicles Plays to America's Competitive Strengths." Information Technology and Innovation Foundation, Washington, D.C., October.

Beland, Louis-Philippe, and Daniel A. Brent. 2017. "Traffic and Crime." Working Paper 2017-02 (Baton Rouge: Louisiana State University, Department of Economics).

Bessen, James. 2015. *Learning by Doing: The Real Connection between Innovation, Wages, and Wealth.* Yale University Press.

Blanco, Myra, Jon Atwood, Sheldon Russell, Timothy Trimble, Julie McClafferty, and Miguel Perez. 2016. *Automated Vehicle Crash Rate Comparison Using Naturalistic Data.* Final Report. Blacksburg, Va.: Virginia Tech Transportation Institute.

Bloom, Nicholas, James Liang, John Roberts, and Zhichun Jenny Ying. 2015. "Does Working from Home Work? Evidence from a Chinese Experiment." *Quarterly Journal of Economics* 130 (February), pp. 165–218.

Blumenauer, Earl. 2016. "Let's Use Self-Driving Cars to Fix America's Busted Infrastructure." *Wired*, May 20.

Bonnefon, Jean-Francois, Azim Shariff, and Lyad Rahwan. 2016. "The Social Dilemma of Autonomous Vehicles." *Science* 352 (June 24), pp. 1573–76.

Bosch, Patrick M., Felix Becker, Henrik Becker, and Kay W. Axhausen. 2018. "Cost-Based Analysis of Autonomous Mobility Services." *Transport Policy* 64 (May), pp. 76–91.

Bowler, Peter J. 2017. *A History of the Future* (Cambridge University Press).

Brown, Edmund G., Jr., Brian P. Kelly, and Malcolm Dougherty. 2014. "California Freight Mobility Plan." Sacramento: California State Transportation Agency, December.

Brueckner, Jan K. 2000. "Urban Sprawl: Diagnosis and Remedies." *International Regional Science Review* 23 (April), pp. 160–71.

Burns, Lawrence D., with Christopher Shulgan. 2018. *Autonomy: The Quest to Build the Driverless Car and How It Will Reshape Our World.* New York: Harper Collins.

California Department of Transportation. 2014. *Transportation Funding in California: 2014.* Report. Sacramento: Division of Transportation Planning, Economic Analysis Branch.

————. 2019. "Truck-Only Lanes." Sacramento: Department of Transportation.

Chetty, Raj, Nathaniel Hendren, Patrick Kline, and Emmanuel Saez. 2014. "Where Is the Land of Opportunity? The Geography of Intergenerational Mobility in the United States." Working Paper 19843 (Cambridge, Mass.: National Bureau of Economic Research), January.

Claudel, Matthew, and Carlo Ratti. 2015. "Full Speed Ahead: How the Driverless Car Could Transform Cities." Washington, D.C.: McKinsey and Company.

Collier, Tina, and Ginger Daniels Goodin. 2002. *The Funding and Financing of Managed Lanes Projects.* Report TX-03/4160-9. Washington, D.C.: U.S. Department of Transportation, Federal Highway Administration, September.

CPCS Transcom. 2015. "Unclogging America's Arteries 2015: Prescriptions for Healthier Highways." Washington, D.C.: American Highway Users Alliance.

Crabbe, Amber E., Rachel Hiatt, Susan D. Poliwka, and Martin Wachs. 2005. "Local Transportation Sales Taxes: California's Experiment in Transportation Finance." *Public Budgeting and Finance* 25 (September), pp. 91–121.

Cutter, W. Bowman, and Sofia F. Franco. 2012. "Do Parking Requirements Significantly Increase the Area Dedicated to Parking? A Test of the Effect of Parking Requirements Values in Los Angeles County." *Transportation Research A* 46 (July), pp. 901–25.

Daziano, Richard A., Mauricio Sarrias, and Benjamin Leard. 2017. "Are Consumers Willing to Pay to Let Cars Drive for Them? Analyzing Response to Autonomous Vehicles." *Transportation Research Part C* 78 (May), pp. 50–164.

Dizikes, Peter. 2012. "Lots of Trouble." MIT *Technology Review News*, June 19.

Downs, Anthony. 1962. "The Law of Peak-Hour Expressway Congestion." *Traffic Quarterly* 16 (July), pp. 393–409.

Duranton, Giles, and Matthew A. Turner. 2011. "The Fundamental Law of Road Congestion: Evidence from U.S. Cities." *American Economic Review* 101 (October), pp. 2616–52.

Duvall, Tyler, Eric Hannon, Jared Katseff, Ben Safran, and Tyler Wallace. 2019. *A New Look at Autonomous-Vehicle Infrastructure*. Report. Washington, D.C.: McKinsey and Company, May.

Edwards, Chris. 2018. "Highways and Gas Tax Diversions." Cato Institute, Washington, D.C., September 19.

Fagnant, Daniel J., and Kara Kockelman. 2015. "Preparing a Nation for Autonomous Vehicles: Opportunities, Barriers, and Policy Recommendations for Capitalizing on Self-Driven Vehicles." *Transportation Research A* 77, pp. 167–81.

Finkelstein, Amy. 2009. "E-ZTAX: Tax Salience and Tax Rates." *Quarterly Journal of Economics* 124 (August), pp. 969–1010.

Ford Motor Company. 2018. *A Matter of Trust: Ford's Approach to Developing Self-Driving Vehicles*. Dearborn, Mich.

Fottrell, Quentin. 2015. "5 Ways Commuting Ruins Your Life." *Market Watch*, September 9.

Fowles, Richard, and Peter D. Loeb. 2018. "Sturdy Inference and the Amelioration Potential for Driverless Cars: The Reduction of Motor Vehicle Fatalities due to Technology." In *Transportation Policy and Economic Regulation*, edited by John Bitzan and James Peoples. Amsterdam: Elsevier Press.

Freemark, Yonah, Anne Hudson, and Jinhua Zhao. 2019. "Are Cities Prepared for Autonomous Vehicles?" *Journal of the American Planning Association* 85, no. 2 (May), pp. 135–51.

Gabbe, C. J., and Greg Pierce. 2017. "Hidden Costs and Deadweight Losses: Bundled Parking and Residential Rents in the Metropolitan United States." *Housing Policy Debate* 27 (August), pp. 219–29.

Gallen, Trevor, and Clifford Winston. 2018. "Transportation Capital and Its Effects on the U.S. Economy: A General Equilibrium Approach." Unpublished paper.

Geistfeld, Mark A. 2018. "A Roadmap for Autonomous Vehicles: State

Tort Liability, Automobile Insurance, and Federal Safety Regulation." *California Law Review* 105, no. 6 (December), pp. 1611–94.

Giarratana, Chris. 2018. "The Job Market and Driverless Cars." Traffic Safety Store, September 24, https://www.trafficsafetystore.com/blog/driverless-cars-will-create-jobs-in-these-6-industries/

Gill, Vijay, Barrie Kirk, Paul Godsmark, and Brian Flemming. 2015. "Automated Vehicles: The Coming of the Next Disruptive Technology." Report. Ottawa: Conference Board of Canada.

Glaeser, Edward L. 2011. *Triumph of the City: How Our Greatest Invention Makes Us Richer, Smarter, Greener, Healthier, and Happier.* New York: Penguin Press.

Glaeser, Edward L., and Joshua L. Gottlieb. 2009. "The Wealth of Cities: Agglomeration Economies and the Spatial Equilibrium in the United States." *Journal of Economic Literature* 47 (December), pp. 983–1028.

Glaeser, Edward L., and Bryce A. Ward. 2009. "The Causes and Consequences of Land Use Regulation: Evidence from Greater Boston." *Journal of Urban Economics* 65 (May), pp. 265–78.

Gordon, Robert J. 2016. *The Rise and Fall of American Economic Growth: The U.S. Standard of Living since the Civil War.* Princeton University Press.

Graehler, Michael, Jr., Richard Alexander Mucci, and Gregory D. Erhardt. 2019. "Understanding the Recent Transit Ridership Decline in Major U.S. Cities: Service Cuts or Emerging Modes?" Paper prepared for the Ninety-Eighth Annual Meeting of the Transportation Research Board.

Harrison, David. 2017. "Speed Limits on Trump's Infrastructure Drive: Federal Laws, Rare Species, and Nimbys." *Wall Street Journal*, February 12.

Herkenhoff, Kyle F., Lee E. Ohanian, and Edward C. Prescott. 2018. "Tarnishing the Golden and Empire States: Land-Use Regulation and the U.S. Economic Slowdown." *Journal of Monetary Economics* 93 (January), pp. 89–109.

Holguin-Veras, José, David Sackey, Sajjad Hussain, and Victor Ochieng. 2003. "Economic and Financial Feasibility of Truck Toll Lanes." *Transportation Research Record: Journal of the Transportation Research Board* 1833 (January), pp. 66–72.

Howard, Phoebe Wall, and Greg Gardner. 2017. "Ford to Build Electric Vehicles in Mexico, Revamp Flat Rock Plant for Self-Driving Cars." *Detroit Free Press*, December 7.

Hsieh, Chang-Tai, and Enrico Moretti. 2018. "Housing Constraints and Spatial Misallocation." *American Economics Journal: Macroeconomics* 11, no. 2 (April), pp. 1–39.

Huet-Vaughn, Emiliano. 2019. "Stimulating the Vote: ARRA Road Spending and Vote Share." *American Economic Journal: Economic Policy* 11 (February), pp. 292–316.

Hymel, Kent. 2009. "Does Traffic Congestion Reduce Employment Growth?" *Journal of Urban Economics* 65 (March), 127–35.

International Transport Forum. 2015. *Urban Mobility System Upgrade: How Shared Self-Driving Cars Could Change City Traffic*. Paris: OECD.

———. 2017. *Managing the Transition to Driverless Road Freight Transport*. Paris: OECD.

Istrate, Emilia, Anya Nowakowski, and Kavita Mak. 2014. *The Road Ahead: County Transportation Funding and Financing*. Report. Washington, D.C.: National Association of Counties.

Jones, Charles I. 2016. "Life and Growth." *Journal of Political Economy* 124 (April), pp. 539–78.

Kahneman, Daniel, and Alan B. Krueger. 2006. "Developments in the Measurement of Subjective Well-Being." *Journal of Economic Perspectives* 20 (Winter), pp. 3–24.

Kalra, Nidhi, and David G. Groves. 2017. *The Enemy of Good: Estimating the Cost of Waiting for Nearly Perfect Autonomous Vehicles*. Santa Monica, Calif.: RAND Corporation.

Kalra, Nidhi, and Susan M. Paddock. 2016. *Driving to Safety: How Many Miles of Driving Would It Take to Demonstrate Autonomous Vehicle Reliability?* Report RR-1478-RC. Santa Monica, Calif.: RAND Corporation.

Kane, Joseph, and Adie Tomer. 2018. "How Big Could the AV Industry Be? 9.5 Million Workers and Counting." Brookings Institution, Metropolitan Infrastructure Initiative, November 15.

Kazi, Khurram, Ravil Bikmetov, Churlzu Lim, M. Yasin Akhtar Raja, and Adam Kelsey. 2018. "Secure, Resilient, and Safety Critical Architecture of Charging Stations for Unsupervised Autonomous Vehicles." Paper prepared for Twenty-First International Conference on Intelligent Transportation Systems, November.

Kerry, Cameron F., and Jack Karsten. 2017. *Gauging Investment in Self-Driving Cars*. Report. Brookings Institution, October.

Knittel, Christopher R., Douglas L. Miller, and Nicholas J. Sanders. 2016. "Caution, Drivers! Children Present: Traffic, Pollution, and Infant Health." *Review of Economics and Statistics* 98, no. 2 (May), pp. 350–66.

Kohler, William J., and Alex Colbert-Taylor. 2015. "Current Law and Potential Legal Issues Pertaining to Automated, Autonomous, and Connected Vehicles." *Santa Clara High Technology Law Journal* 31 (January), pp. 99–138.

Krugman, Paul. 2009. "The Increasing Returns Revolution in Trade and Geography." *American Economic Review* 99 (June), pp. 561–71.

Lamotte, Raphaël, André de Palma, and Nicholas Geroliminis. 2017. "On the Use of Reservation-Based Autonomous Vehicles for Demand Management." *Transportation Research Part B* 99 (May), pp. 205–27.

Langer, Ashley, Vikram Maheshri, and Clifford Winston. 2017. "From Gallons to Miles: A Disaggregate Analysis of Automobile Travel and Externality Taxes." *Journal of Public Economics* 152 (August), pp. 34–46.

Langer, Ashley, and Clifford Winston. 2008. "Toward a Comprehensive Assessment of Road Pricing Accounting for Land Use." In *Brookings-Wharton Papers on Urban Affairs: 2008*, edited by Gary Burtless and Janet Rothenberg Pack, pp. 127–75. Brookings Institution Press.

LaReau, James L. 2019. "GM's Global Gamble to Fund a Big Bet on the Future." *Detroit Free Press*, February 21.

Lehe, Lewis. 2019. "Downtown Congestion Pricing in Practice." *Transportation Research Part C: Emerging Technologies* 100 (March), pp. 200–23.

Li, Shanjun, Joshua Linn, and Erich Muehlegger. 2014. "Gasoline Taxes and Consumer Behavior." *American Economic Journal: Economic Policy* 6 (November), pp. 302–42.

Light, Thomas. 2007. "Time-Use Approach for Estimating Commuters' Value of Travel Time." Paper prepared for Transportation Research Board Eighty-Sixth Annual Meeting, Washington, D.C., January 21–25.

Lindsey, Robin. 2006. "Do Economists Reach a Conclusion on Road Pricing? The Intellectual History of an Idea." *Econ Journal Watch* 3, May, pp. 292–379.

Litman, Todd. 2019. "Autonomous Vehicle Implementation Predictions: Implications for Transport Planning." Victoria Transport Policy Institute, Victoria, Canada, March 18.

MacDuffie, John Paul. 2018. "The Policy Trajectories of Autonomous Vehicles." *Wharton Policy Initiative* 6 (May).

Mack, Eric. 2018. "New MIT Systems Lets Self-Driving Cars go Almost Anywhere." *Forbes*, May 7.

McDonnell, Simon, Josiah Madar, and Vicki Been. 2011. "Minimum Parking Requirements and Housing Affordability in New York City." *Housing Policy Debate* 21, no. 1 (December), pp. 45–68.

McKinnon, Alan C. 2005. "The Economic and Environmental Benefits of Increasing Maximum Truck Weight: The British Experience." *Transportation Research Part D* 10 (January), pp. 77–95.

Melo, Patrick C., Daniel J. Graham, and Ruben Brage-Ardao. 2013. "The Productivity of Transport Infrastructure Investment: A Meta-Analysis of Empirical Evidence." *Regional Science and Urban Economics* 43 (September), pp. 695–706.

Milakis, Dimitris, Maaike Snedler, Bart van Arem, Bert van Wee, and Goncalo Homem de Almeida Correia. 2017. "Development and Transport Implications of Autonomous Vehicles in the Netherlands: Scenarios for 2030 and 2050." *European Journal of Transport and Infrastructure Research* 17 (January), pp. 63–85.

Miller, Cheryl. 2017. "Federal, State Officials Face Sharp Curves in Regulating Driverless Cars." *National Law Journal*, May 1.

Mohring, Herbert, and Mitchell Harwitz. 1962. *Highway Benefits: An Analytical Framework*. Northwestern University Press.

Munnell, Alicia H. 1990. "Why Has Productivity Growth Declined? Productivity and Public Investment." *New England Economic Review* (January/February), pp. 3–22.

Mutschler, Ann Steffora. 2018. "Connected Cars: From Chip to City." *Semiconductor Engineering*, November 1.

National Transportation Operations Coalition. 2007. *Executive Summary: 2007 National Traffic Signal Report Card*. Washington, D.C.

NHTSA (National Highway Traffic Safety Administration). 2015. *The Economic and Societal Impact of Motor Vehicle Crashes, 2010 (Revised)*. Washington, D.C.: U.S. Department of Transportation.

Nourinejad, Medhi, Sina Bahrami, and Matthew J. Roorda. 2018. "Designing Parking Facilities for Autonomous Vehicles." *Transportation Research Part B: Methodological* 109, pp. 110–27.

Ostrovsky, Michael, and Michael Schwarz. 2018. "Carpooling and the Economics of Self-Driving Cars." Working paper (Stanford, Calif.: Stanford Graduate School of Business), February.

Pigou, Arthur C. 1920. *The Economics of Welfare.* London: Macmillan Press.

Prud'homme, Remy, and Chang-Woon Lee. 1999. "Size, Sprawl, Speed, and the Efficiency of Cities." *Urban Studies* 36 (October), pp. 1849–58.

Puga, Diego. 2010. "The Magnitude and Causes of Agglomeration Economies." *Journal of Regional Science* 50 (February), pp. 203–19.

Quain, John R. 2019. "These High-Tech Sensors May Be the Key to Autonomous Cars." *New York Times*, September, 26.

Ranaiefar, Fatemah. 2014. "A Structural Direct Demand Model for Interregional Commodity Flow Forecasting." Ph.D. diss., University of California, Irvine.

Ranaiefar, Fatemeh, Joseph Y. J. Chow, Daniel Rodriguez-Roman, Pedro V. Carmargo, and Stephen G. Ritchie. 2012. "Geographic Scalability and Supply Chain Elasticity of a Structural Commodity Generation Model Using Public Data." *Transportation Research Record: Journal of the Transportation Research Board* 2378, pp. 73–83.

Ranft, Florian, Martin Adler, Patrick Diamond, Eugenia Guerrero, and Matthew Laza. 2016. *Freeing the Road: Shaping the Future for Autonomous Vehicles.* Report. London: Policy Network Publication, November.

Ratner, Stephen. 2018. "Taxation of Autonomous Vehicles in Cities and States." *Tax Lawyer* 71 (Summer), pp. 1051–76.

Regional Plan Association. 2017. *New Mobility: Autonomous Vehicles and the Region.* New York, October.

Robyn, Dorothy. 2015. "It's Time to Corporatize Air Traffic Control (the Right Way)." Brookings Institution, September.

Rohlin, Shawn M., and Jeffrey P. Thompson. 2018. "Local Sales Taxes, Employment, and Tax Competition." *Regional Science and Urban Economics* 70 (May), pp. 373–83.

Royal Society for Public Health. 2017. *Health in a Hurry.* Report. London, August.

SAFE (Securing America's Future Energy). 2018. "America's Workforce and the Self-Driving Future." Washington, D.C., June.

Santos, Georgina. 2005. "Urban Congestion Charging: A Comparison between London and Singapore." *Transport Reviews* 25, no. 5, pp. 511–34.

Schwartz, Samuel I. 2018. "How Autonomous Vehicles Will Shape Our World." *Wall Street Journal*, October 18.

Shatz, Howard J., Karin E. Kitchens, Sandra Rosenbloom, and Martin

Wachs. 2011. *Highway Infrastructure and the Economy: Implications for Federal Policy*. Santa Monica, Calif.: RAND Corporation.

Shirley, Chad, and Clifford Winston. 2004. "Firm Inventory Behavior and the Returns from Highway Infrastructure Investments." *Journal of Urban Economics* 55 (March), pp. 398–415.

Shoup, Donald C. 2005. *The High Cost of Free Parking*. Chicago: Planners Press.

———. 2018. "Truth in Transportation Planning." In *Parking and the City*, edited by Donald C. Shoup, pp. 59–73. Abingdon, U.K.: Routledge.

Sidders, Jack, and Jess Shankleman. 2018. "A Driverless Future Threatens the Laws of Real Estate." *Bloomberg News*, February 5.

Siddiqui, Faiz. 2019. "Silicon Valley Pioneered Self-Driving Cars. But Some of its Tech-Savvy Residents Don't Want Them Tested in Their Neighborhoods." *Washington Post*, October 3.

Simeonova, Emilia, Janet Currie, Peter Nilsson, and Reed Walker. 2018. "Congestion Pricing, Air Pollution, and Children's Health." Working Paper 24410 (Cambridge, Mass.: National Bureau of Economic Research), March.

Simoni, Michele D., Kara M. Kockelman, Krishna M. Gurumurthy, and Joschka Bischoff. 2018. "Congestion Pricing in a World of Self-Driving Vehicles: An Analysis of Different Strategies in Alternative Future Scenarios." Working paper. Cornell University.

Small, Kenneth A., and Erik T. Verhoef. 2007. *The Economics of Urban Transportation*. Abingdon, U.K.: Routledge.

Small, Kenneth A., and Clifford Winston. 1988. "Optimal Highway Durability." *American Economic Review* 78 (June), pp. 560–69.

Small, Kenneth A., Clifford Winston, and Carol A. Evans. 1989. *Road Work: A New Highway Pricing and Investment Policy*. Brookings Institution Press.

Small, Kenneth A., Clifford Winston, and Jia Yan. 2005. "Uncovering the Distribution of Motorists' Preferences for Travel Time and Reliability." *Econometrica* 73 (July), pp. 1367–82.

Smart, Michael J., and Nicholas J. Klein. 2015. *A Longitudinal Analysis of Cars, Transit, and Employment Outcomes*. Report 12-49. San Jose, Calif.: San Jose State University, Mineta National Transit Research Consortium.

Smith, Bryant Walker. 2017. "Automated Driving and Product Liability." *Michigan State Law Review* 1, pp. 1–74.

Snyder, Tanya. 2018. "What Went Wrong with New Orleans Transit?" *Politico*, November 20.

Sweet, Matthias. 2014. "Traffic Congestion's Economic Impacts: Evidence from U.S. Metropolitan Regions." *Urban Studies* 51, no. 10 (June), pp. 2088–110.

Tomer, Adie. 2012. "Where the Jobs Are: Employer Access to Labor by Transit." Brookings Institution, Metropolitan Policy Program.

TRIP (The Road Information Program). 2016. "Key Facts about America's Surface Transportation System and Federal Funding." Washington, D.C.

U.S. Department of Transportation. 2017. *Automated Driving Systems 2.0: A Vision for Safety,*

———. 2018. *Preparing for the Future of Transportation 3.0.*

Van den Berg, Vincent A. C., and Erik. T. Verhoef. 2016. "Autonomous Cars and Dynamic Bottleneck Congestion: The Effects on Capacity, Value of Time, and Preference Heterogeneity." *Transportation Research. Part B* 94 (December), pp. 43–60.

Vickrey, William. 1963. "Pricing in Urban and Suburban Transport." *American Economic Review* 53 (May), pp. 452–65.

———. 1969. "Congestion Theory and Transport Investment." *American Economic Review* 59 (May), pp. 251–60.

Viscelli, Steve. 2018. *Driverless? Autonomous Trucks and the Future of the American Trucker.* Report. Berkeley: University of California, UC Berkeley Labor Center, September.

Walters, Alan A. 1961. "The Theory and Measurement of Private and Social Cost of Highway Congestion." *Econometrica* 29 (October), pp. 676–99.

Wartzman, Rick. 2017. "The First Time America Freaked Out over Automation." *Politico*, May 30.

Waymo. 2017. *On the Road to Fully Self-Driving.* Waymo Safety Report. Mountain View, Calif.

Wenderoth, Michael C. 2018. "Why This Country (Not the USA) Will be First to Adopt Driverless Cars." *Forbes*, May 31.

Winston, Clifford. 1991. "Efficient Transportation Infrastructure Policy." *Journal of Economic Perspectives* 5 (Winter), pp. 113–27.

————. 2013. "On the Performance of the U.S. Transportation System: Caution Ahead." *Journal of Economic Literature* 51 (September), pp. 773–824.

————. 2019. *Gaining Ground: Markets Helping Government*, Brookings Institution, unpublished book manuscript.

Winston, Clifford, and Ashley Langer. 2006. "The Effect of Government Highway Spending on Road Users' Congestion Costs." *Journal of Urban Economics* 60 (November), 463–83.

Winston, Clifford, and Vikram Maheshri. 2007. "On the Social Desirability of Urban Rail Transit." *Journal of Urban Economics* 62 (September), pp. 362–82.

Winston, Clifford, and Fred Mannering. 2014. "Implementing Technology to Improve Public Highway Performance: A Leapfrog Technology from the Private Sector Is Going to Be Necessary." *Economics of Transportation* 3 (June), pp. 158–65.

Winston, Clifford, and Chad Shirley. 1998. *Alternate Route: Toward Efficient Urban Transportation*. Brookings Institution Press.

Winston, Clifford, and Jia Yan. 2011. "Can Privatization of U.S. Highways Improve Motorists' Welfare?" *Journal of Public Economics* 95 (August), pp. 993–1005.

Work Zone Management Program. 2016. "Facts and Statistics—Work Zone Mobility." Federal Highway Administration, March 2.

Wu, Cathy, Aboudy Kreidieh, Kanaad Parvate, Eugene Vinitsky, and Alexandre M. Bayen, "Flow: A Modular Learning Framework for Autonomy in Traffic," Berkeley Mobile Sensing Lab, submitted October 16, 2017, last revised October 1, 2019, https://bayen.berkeley.edu/down loads/flow-project.

Yankelevich, Aleksandr, R. V. Rikard, Travis Kadylak, Michael J. Hall, Elizabeth A. Mack, John P. Verboncoeur, and Shelia R. Cotten. 2018. "Preparing the Workforce for Automated Vehicles." American Center for Mobility, July 30.

Zakharenko, Roman. 2016. "Self-Driving Cars Will Change Cities." *Regional Science and Urban Economics* 61 (November), pp. 26–37.

Index